Discovering
NATURAL
HORSEMANSHIP

Discovering
NATURAL
HORSEMANSHIP

A Beginner's Odyssey

Tom Moates

THE LYONS PRESS
Guilford, Connecticut
AN IMPRINT OF THE GLOBE PEQUOT PRESS

The Lyons Press is an imprint of The Globe Pequot Press

"Feeling of a Horse" was originally published in a slightly different form in
Eclectic Horseman magazine, in issue 23, May/June 2005.

Parts of "Naming My Two" and "Whipper Tears His Eye" appeared in case report
and essay forms in *Equus* magazine, in issue 331, May 2005.

Parts of "Going Barefoot" appeared in a different form as a cover article in *Natural
Horse* magazine, in volume 6-issue 6, 2004.

10 9 8 7 6 5 4 3 2 1

Printed in the United States of America

Designed by Maggie Peterson

ISBN-13: 978-1-59228-950-9

ISBN-10: 1-59228-950-9

Library of Congress Cataloging-in-Publication data is available on file.

This book is dedicated to those whose stories are so entwined with my own that our very roots commingle below the surface, closest to the source: Carol, and the horses, Niji, Sokeri, and Whipper Snapper.

CONTENTS

FOREWORD

IT'S BEEN LESS THAN A YEAR since my first call from Tom Moates. I'd been warned by a mutual friend that he might call. The reason for his call was to get my comments for a magazine article. It didn't take long to realize Tom was a beginner in this horsemanship journey. I was impressed with his honesty about how much of a beginner he was. But then I was even more impressed with his eagerness to learn more.

In the communication Tom and I had over the next several months it came out that he was writing a book. *Another book on horsemanship*, I thought. The stores are full of books and videos on the subject. I wasn't so sure we needed another one. As my understanding of Tom's mission with this book grew so did my curiosity. I have just finished reading the book you hold in your hands, and no, it's not just another book on horsemanship. Tom has done a great job of giving us a glimpse of his journey in this quest for better horsemanship. No advice—no "how-to." Just a good, honest account of a beginner's journey.

It is easy to lose track of our "beginnings" at anything as it unfolds deeper and becomes part of our way of life. Sometimes the experience and the language become so much a part of us we fail to realize why anyone else doesn't understand. And yet those at the beginning certainly struggle.

Having now met Tom face to face and spent a little time getting to know him, I have an idea of what makes him such a good writer. I believe it is his great desire to share with others what he has come to understand is involved in this journey—which makes me thankful for his passion to keep learning so he can continue to share more of his journey with the rest of us.

I personally thank Tom for sharing his experiences as a beginner. Tom gives other beginners in this quest plenty to relate to, but he also takes those of us who have never known a life without horses back to revisit some of the perils, struggles, and lifechanging discoveries that horses present all of us.

Harry Whitney

June 2006

ACKNOWLEDGMENTS

WITHOUT A DOUBT, downstage center, spotlights please—
Jessie Shiers deserves applause for her work on this book (take a
bow, Jessie). I am forever grateful for those heroic hours she
spent, as the editor on this project, not only picking at my prose,
but tolerating the full-on assault of my rather zealous personality when it comes to horses and writing. Her efforts are worthy
of a mention *and* a medal.

The first person in the chain of events that became this book
is Stephanie von Hirschberg, my agent and friend. I'm certain
events would not have unfolded as they did for this work to get
produced and in print if she hadn't been just offstage in the
wings providing direction from before the writing began,
through all the twists and turns, up to this very day. I'm very
grateful for all she's done.

The next, first person in the unfolding of this book's creation
is another friend, and editor, Emily Kitching. Emily initially put
me in touch with The Lyons Press, for which I'm extremely grateful, and it is she who has designed and developed the website for
this book (www.TomMoates.com) along with her partner in life
and at Eclectic Horseman Communications, Steve Bell.

Arika Legg, Rainey Houston, Ken Moates, and Melissa
Moates all helped Carol get the images to help tell this story.

Thanks for all their hard work and the time it took from getting the photos taken to their final destination, as well as putting energy into the book in other ways.

Many other people are linked to the creation of this book, but let me especially mention my thanks to those that were instrumental in ways like reading early versions of many chapters, giving their advice at various points along the way, and bearing the brunt of me being a colossal nuisance: Christine Barakat, Diana Johnson, Linda Parelli, Randi Peters, Harry Whitney, Dr. David Williams, and Terrie Wood.

INTRODUCTION

WRITING AND FARMING are all I've ever really wanted to do for a living. Since childhood I've worked at both. A thousand-acre dairy farm was my home growing up, so I got in plenty of farming experience. By the time I was an adolescent, I had set my sights on the most brilliant, most inebriated writer role models and worked hard to follow in their footsteps. Managing somehow to survive to the ripe old age of eighteen, I ended up in treatment for my pursuits, got sober, stayed sober, and went to college to get a degree in writing.

Throughout the time since college, I've worked as a professional stagehand, a traditional building specialist, and as a renewable energy specialist. I'll spare the details of the insanity it takes to dovetail all that into a life of work. Suffice it to say that the writing always held the highest career priority, but the other work afforded me time enough to continue serious writing. The by-product of this situation was that I ended up a leading writer in the subjects of renewable energy and homestead living and building. But, while I passionately pursued writing (getting up before dawn to work on whatever I had going at any given moment, including stabs at fiction and children's books), the subjects I could get published often felt less exciting to me than the work of writing. Something was missing. As time went on, and I had covered every angle of the regular fare multiple times, re-hashing the topics over and over again became like wading around in really smelly waist-deep mud.

When my wife's gelding Niji came into my life and my dormant passion for horses began to surface, an overwhelming desire to combine writing with this new infatuation gripped me. There was a problem, though. Even though I could claim an impressive writing resume, I lacked *any* expertise on the subject of horses. This alone could easily thwart my attempts to break into the equine magazine market. So, with years of practice trying to bust into different magazines, and the enormous heap of rejection and acceptance letters to prove it, I began to develop article ideas that didn't require me being an expert, ones that were based on research, interviews, or my personal experience as a beginner with horses, and query various magazines.

I'm a pretty tenacious writer. One might say I'm unrealistically hopeful when it comes to seeing my future in this field. With confidence I can tell you if I were looking at this profession simply as a job like I do stage work or electrical work, I never would have made it this far. It's too rough a roller coaster and can make you sick.

There is, however, sometimes in people a drive to do something that propels them forward even when no clear path is cut through life's wilderness to show the way. There is no guarantee that there even really is a way, or a place to get to. It is all a hunch, and the only compass reading the direction to it is the one in your gut. Joe Campbell called it "following your bliss." Some call it foolish. I feel a desire to pursue writing so strongly that I fear what my life would be like without it—that I might just die. Without warning, I found myself feeling this same crazy intensity about getting better with horses. The two combined verged on overwhelming. It was the brink of obsession overload. Then came misfortune.

My mare's foal Whipper Snapper had a terrible accident, and the events that followed took a toll on me. I lost twenty pounds that month; it would take a year to gain it back. Being present from the beginning of this beautiful, perfectly healthy colt's life, witnessing the injury, spending the next month with a crazy barn schedule, and worrying about his health chipped away at my serenity. Once the worst of the danger was past, I began to relax and felt the need to share the story with other horse folk who might understand the intensity of my experience. So, I spent a few weeks getting it all down, even returning to speak with the resident surgeon, Dr. Graham Keys, DVM, at Virginia Tech, to get all the technical details correct, and sent it to Christine Barakat at *Equus*.

It's funny how so many aspects of horses in my life are doors flinging open to new opportunities. Serendipity came riding into my life on Niji's back and has chosen to stay awhile. Fresh air and sunlight of this new world entered the dank, stagnant areas of my life, long in need of spring cleaning. When I finally heard from Christine for the first time, she was very pleased with the piece, as were the other editors. The article was accepted right away, and, to my exhilaration, she asked if she could assign me another case report. As a freelancer, getting an assignment from an awesome magazine is the coup de grace—they give you an idea and the contacts, sometimes cover the expenses of working on the piece, and it's a sure thing. It had only happened to me a couple of times before in my whole career. This was a very good sign.

These two case reports immediately snowballed in the next few months into two features, an essay, several more case reports, and a "True Tale." After writing for *Equus* for about a year, I even received the title of contributing writer with my own spot in the masthead. Not only has *Equus* been a perfect fit for my aspirations as a professional writer in the equine area, but the work I do for them has broadened my knowledge base on the subject of horses in a tremendous way. No part of this has been more profound than my conversations with the medical editor, Dr. Matthew Mackay-Smith, DVM. Every time we speak my brain creaks with the stretching caused by new information being packed in. The man is an encyclopedia on two legs and a fantastic resource to have on your side if you are an equine writer. Whipper's accident may be the best example I've ever experienced of a seriously horrible unfortunate event leading to a series of miraculously brilliant events providing a tremendous opportunity for a positive outcome.

Equine writing became so prominent in my life so quickly that in the first four months after writing that case report on Whipper Snapper, I placed and wrote more horse articles than I usually can get together in all other subjects combined in two or three years! It was nothing less than an explosion. It became so incredible that editors I'd never heard of from national horse magazines I'd never contacted were contacting *me* out of the blue to assign me articles. My brother puts my equine writing success pretty accurately when he says, "You're an overnight sensation, Bro . . . it only took you twenty years!"

This book was well underway by this time. Enough experiences had piled up even early on in my adventures with horses and the Better Way to begin to form in my mind a book about the honest plight of the beginner. And this snowball has rolled steadily ever since. Becoming a regular contributor to many horse publications has allowed me to focus on horses without the sidetracking of energy necessary to break into new markets. Most importantly, I have an outlet to pour my heart into like never before. This is really where the success comes from. That passion I possess for both horses and writing, along with a lot of writing experience, just comes through in between the lines. I haven't written an article on horses yet where I didn't learn lessons. Getting the opportunity to share these personal lessons with others feels like a great gift in my life rather than work. I find myself wishing I didn't require sleep so I could keep writing about horses, or riding horses for that matter.

It's a strange thing to find such an overwhelming infatuation in life as I did with horses at thirty-five. It seemed to me quite late for a passion like this to take hold; I would have guessed, with horses in particular, the average person would have it gripping his heart at about age nine. However, I learn with each clinic I attend that I am hardly alone. The truth is that quite a few people are coming to horses and natural horsemanship later in life. I know a few that started in their fifties. Regardless of age, a sincerity and joy can come to people through working in a good way with horses; it transcends age because it is about personal growth, and I don't think a horse cares how old a person is.

Horses have so much to offer people. I'm always amazed at how unconditionally they are willing to share with us. Especially when we try to work with them with kindness and see things "from the horse's point of view," as clinician Harry Whitney says. We must open up and try to uncover the layers that allow us to approach horses in a way that not only produces positive results from the viewpoint of training and what the horse mechanically does with his body, but brings our horses to a better place inside themselves as well. I'm still getting better at this, and with every achievement, I clearly see a new set of challenges. The journey of natural horsemanship ultimately is about changing the human. The horse remains a horse, doing what he has been capable of doing all along. We, however, can learn to change in ways that allow our horses to become less bothered. We can present requests in ways that horses understand, and that clarity helps them in our relationship to one another. We can make it better for them in this human-dominated world.

This is the story of the very beginning of a journey, one that already is somewhere further along for me. This is, however, a book I wish I could have read when I started out. I think there are many points that can provide some clarity for the beginner, some I wish I hadn't found out the hard way. It is also a story that probably resonates with anyone at any point along the natural horsemanship trail.

The first sentence of the book reflects a moment that was like a seed sprouting. Before it, I was lying in the compost of life on a completely horseless path, minding my own business, trying to figure out my mid-thirties—after that moment, the seed sprouted, took root, and found plenty of nourishment from my past to grow vigorously. And everything changed, forever.

CHAPTER ONE

NIJI

"QUARTER HORSE, AMISH TRAINED," read the classified ad in the local paper one July a few years back. It caught Carol's eye. Given my wife's history, the fact that she even glanced at it, let alone connected with it, was serendipitous.

"Amish trained" is what grabbed her. Knowing now her relationship with this gelding named Niji, it probably could have read "trained by crazed brute" and the two of them would have found one another anyway, so strong is the gravity of the connection that pulled them to each other across space and time. The key, though, to all that has since transpired with us and horses was foreshadowed in her understanding (or misunderstanding) of "Amish trained."

To Carol it meant trained in a gentle, kind, and respectful way. Really, we have no idea what it actually meant, even now after inquiring about it. Several things are certain, though. The ad drew Carol to the horse that has brought her tremendous healing. Carol had spent years in the mainstream horse world in her earlier life before we met. If horses were to return to her life now she was looking for a better way. "Amish" hinted at what she must have sensed lay ahead, because soon it was "natural horsemanship" that she and Niji discovered. And I suddenly veered off my horseless course in life and rather quickly became thirsty to get to know horses and this gentle way of building a positive relationship with them.

Carol even thinking about looking at a horse spoke volumes. In a divorce years earlier, she had lost all of her horses—a herd of seven. These were mostly Paints, which, at the time, weren't easy to come by in Virginia. She had worked for years breeding and selling Quarter Horses to be able to go out of state and buy a good Paint mare. Then she had spent several years building up her stock, which she was forced to leave behind. If that wasn't enough to keep horses blocked from her psyche, a Paint foal that she hand-fed for weeks because the mare had no milk ran into a sharp branch from a recently limbed tree while playing in a pasture, pierced its chest, and bled to death. These were Grand Canyons cut across her heart by the runoff of torrential downpours of distress, unending sadness to be sorted out in the afterlife, if possible even then.

Niji, however, chose to come sooner—much sooner. Carol, to my surprise, opened her heart to him. She started to share some positive stories from her past of working with horses, but she also began to express that she felt there must be a better way available to her than before. Carol wasn't specific, and I never pried into this part of her life, but that "Amish trained" line from the ad definitely signified to her a different direction she now wanted to follow with horses.

My brother and his wife came to visit on July 4th that year. Ken is in the Navy and usually comes out to the mountains to visit at least twice a year, but this was the first time Melissa had ventured down with him. So strong was the force pulling Carol to Niji that she worried in a fairly panicked way someone else might get the horse before we had the chance—a curious reaction from a person who had barely mentioned horses to me in over a decade of marriage and who had not been considering getting a horse. With some misgivings, we asked our freshly arrived guests if they would mind our going out for a little while to have a look at this gelding. They didn't, and the whole out-of-the-blue event spun its own course.

Carol's nervousness and anticipation were uncharacteristic. I was always ready to add to the animal collection—goat, hogs, a 200-pound Mastiff, two 150-pound Mastiff/Ridgeback crosses. The bigger the better, as far as I was concerned. But for Carol, going to look at a horse, let alone one for *sale*, was big medicine.

Winding through gravel Blue Ridge back roads, we finally came to a barren field with an aging barbed wire fence that held a fiery red horse, a color I soon learned was sorrel. We got out of the car, met the owner—a jolly single woman with two kids and two other horses pastured on another farm to care for—and went up to Niji. Aside from needing some groceries and having a few nicks from leaning into the wire, he was magnificent.

Fluid movement. Big expressive eyes. Dish face. Short frame and flagged tail when he cantered about. I would learn from Carol that these characteristics most likely indicated Arabian blood mixed with the Quarter Horse he was advertised to be.

Niji's name, the owner explained, is the Ojibwa word for "friend." Such a name in the Blue Ridge Mountains of southwest Virginia, a thousand miles southeast of Ojibwa territory, where Native Americans are seldom encountered, was one more curious piece of this strange puzzle. It was, however, no more odd than the unforeseen consequences that would arrive along with that broadening of our vocabulary. It was at once a door opening and a stepping across the threshold of the unknown, with the door just as quickly closing behind and locking forever. That day changed everything.

Niji was led from the paddock, and a boy started a push mower and ran it near him to demonstrate his stability around such noises. *Odd*, I thought, *But hey, steady is good*. It was a hot day, and the owner brought Niji into the shade of a tree by the house. Niji didn't mind being fooled with, tacked up, or rubbed most places. Mostly he grabbed at mouthfuls of grass, gobbling up all he could from the lawn. The owner and her daughter saddled him and Carol got on. She had little luck trying to get him to walk from the driver's seat. The owner led him by the bit while Carol, from the saddle, felt him move underneath her. Obviously he wasn't well trained under saddle, but he was well behaved. More importantly, Carol sensed his huge heart under those muscles and knew this horse had potential for her. They connected at some deep level immediately. The invisible force that brought Carol to Niji intensified through contact. The onlooker may never have noticed a change in her, but I knew. I *felt* the intensity of her connection to Niji, coupled with surprise—she was perhaps more shocked to have found a horse for herself at this stage in her life than anybody. In our experiences together, the scene would fall under the heading "surreal." The whole series of events happened quickly and was emotionally charged, making it seem much like a dream. I knew we would be getting him before she ever dismounted and spoke to me about the horse.

We spent more time there than we had planned, with our guests waiting at home. We made a down payment and returned the next day with grain and hay. Thus started two weeks of trips to see and feed Niji almost every day, while I began fencing in part of our land. I worked on it before and after my construction job all week, double-timing on weekends.

The difficult work, expenses, and new responsibilities felt like a missing but perfectly fitting piece of my life had just been restored to its proper place. A large dairy farm in Virginia had been my boyhood home. Horses had been present along the periphery of my whole life, but I never connected with them. I had a few English riding lessons when I was probably eleven—I remember the high boots I wore better than the lessons themselves—and there were a few "kick-to-go, pull-to-stop" rides along the way, which now lie in the dust under the couch of my memory. Around my second year of college I had a short relationship with a woman who owned racehorses, and much of the time we stayed on a small farm with them. Looking back, it seems they lived in box stalls all the time. They were really high strung and not particularly pleasant to hang around, and we only went riding once.

So during the first thirty-odd years of my life, there was little more to my relationship with horses than feeding and mucking these few horses I met along the way. Perhaps the joy I experienced improving our farm and being around Niji was a return to those formative years, when nearly every day I fed and cared for large animals, usually Holstein cows and calves. But something new was at work—horses were a key unlocking something inside me. I wondered why a horse suddenly awoke a passion in me— why now at thirty-five, I began building serious relationships with them when it could have happened at any time with the others I had known along the way. When Niji entered my life, in a day I was on a new course that would soon open more doors than I could have imagined.

Walking up to Niji, sweet as he was, still took courage for me at times. Even with my general love of the large creatures, the newness of being around so big and powerful an animal with such a different mind from bovines created some natural apprehension. I practiced not showing fear while approaching him. Soon, though, it melted away, and I began to trust my new friend. Luckily, he is a horse that thinks humans are fairly okay anyway.

With the fence strung and gates hung, I borrowed the former owner's horse trailer and moved Niji home. He loaded perfectly. He unloaded perfectly. His ears spun all around like radar, and he looked around his new environment curiously with those deep, dark, almond eyes. Then he started eating the clover along the side of the driveway. A good sign, I thought.

At first, I couldn't leave Niji alone. Of course, he was Carol's horse. But I would come up with any excuse to go over and see him. Running my hands along his coat. Breathing in his horse smell. Watching his movements. Exploring what he liked and what worried him. Bothering him at night after dark with a flashlight to "check on him."

Even now, much later, I'm the very same way. Although I now have my own horses to keep tabs on, I can't resist the opportunity to go see what Niji is up to and bury my fingers in his thick mane. Part of his mane flops over to the opposite side of his neck, and I flip it back over in a futile effort to correct it. I scratch his few itchy spots, which Carol found and shared with me, making his nose purse in a funny way. Other new lessons came quickly to me as well, like learning to block his headstrong tendencies—without frustration, just matter-of-factly raising my forearm in a reflex to keep his swinging head from pushing hard against me.

Not long after Niji moved in, Carol discovered what she was looking for in a better way with horses—or perhaps what way was looking for her. Bev Martinkosky—a friend who works at the library, has horses, and was a farrier until recently—mentioned a local woman named Terrie Wood, who is a trainer and works with a method called "natural horsemanship." For Carol and me, the name certainly seemed to fit with other aspects of our life, like organic gardening, medicinal herbalism, and powering the farm and house completely with solar energy. One day soon after, while I was out working, Terrie Wood came to the house and shared some fundamentals with Carol and Niji. She taught some basic groundwork to Carol and showed her with Niji how to get started.

That evening I returned to an excited Carol, who had written down a list of "games" to play with Niji. She explained how within minutes Terrie was showing her how to play with Niji in ways that applied pressure and release and got him to move in desirable ways. After one session, already Carol could lightly touch Niji with her fingertips and he would move for her. She showed me—she touched his flank, and he gently stepped his hind end away from her. Then she came around in front of him, touched him with a few fingers on the chest, and he stepped backwards. I was amazed. I wouldn't have guessed her first experience with Terrie would produce what seemed like refined moves. Carol started to play the games with Niji frequently, and I watched from a distance, fascinated. At this point, although the frame of reference didn't exist yet for me to understand or really talk about it, I had already crossed over to this new stage of life. The gravitational pull of this new heavenly body in my universe had me in its field. My life was changing and my understanding of the world expanding. Sharp turns in life weren't new to me. I'd long ago veered off the major highway of life, with its neat, clearly legible signs, smooth pavement, and mile markers, onto steep mountain trails and twisty gravel roads, with neither a sign nor any clear view of what lay around the next curve. Niji's recent arrival glowed with the aura of such serendipity from the first moment Carol mentioned the ad for the "Amish trained" horse.

The dynamic between Niji and Carol was my first experience of what natural horse folk call "feel." This invisible, nebulous concept (much like "enlightenment," it seems) is what is striven for between human and horse. The various methods and programs offered by the gurus of what I often call the Better Way with horses are rough road maps to this telepathy. Feel can't be defined; it's experiential. It's not really about getting a horse to step here or there or circle on a lead rope, although that's a by-product of it, or a path to it, and often useful in a practical way at times—it's about the space between human and horse disappearing. It's about some psychic connection where the two become one. Carol and Niji shared this on some level right out of the gate of their relationship. I could only watch in wonder, not being in the loop myself.

Niji.

It wasn't long before Carol stopped using the halter and lead rope most of the time when she played with Niji. I was absolutely amazed. There was no way I was going to try it at that point, and I stuck to more conservative lead rope cues when I worked with him. It was fascinating to watch them though; Carol could get Niji to walk or trot by moving along beside him and speeding up or slowing down her walk. She quickly had him jumping barrels laid sideways in the round corral just by asking him with her body language. Carol had figured out how to get Niji to rear when she asked, which came about by accident. She had washed Niji, which was his cue to find a dust bowl to roll in. She beat him to the powdery dirt spot in his paddock and then, while facing him, bent low at the waist, stretched out her arms, and then stood up straight and lifted them way over her head to "shoo" him away. Niji reared. I saw it happening and was shocked, both that he made such an aggressive move and that Carol wasn't the least bit intimidated by his tall frame doing the "high-ho-Silver" right in front of her.

Then she did it again, and so did he. They were having fun! Afterwards, she could get him into it pretty easy. I never tried that one.

On another day, Carol was playing fetch with the dogs, using a tennis ball outside around the gardens. Niji was watching intently from the other side of his fence, so she wondered . . . *Hmm.* I watched as she got the tennis ball, climbed into the paddock, and approached the gelding. Niji was already intrigued and eagerly checked out the bright ball in her hand, probably to see if it was a Golden Delicious. When she tossed it a distance, his natural curiosity soared and he spun and went after it. The very first time, he snorted at it and picked it up in his mouth. Carol had to go over to him to get the ball from his mouth. After a few more throws with her calling him, though, he actually picked up the ball and returned to her. It wasn't a completely consistent game, but many times she was quite successful with full revolutions of the fetch cycle, start to finish.

It was all great fun to Carol, who was both really creative at having fun with her horse and fearless. At that time, however, I would have been way too scared to work "at liberty" as some call it, up close with a horse, let alone be in front of a rearing horse without a lead. Their trust and connection shined.

I was, however, absolutely, completely, and hopelessly hooked. Horses had landed in my world, and luckily so did an awareness of and link to the Better Way with them right at the beginning. Thus began my odyssey with natural horsemanship, all thanks to Carol and Niji.

CHAPTER TWO

DISCOVERING NATURAL HORSEMANSHIP

I SUPPOSE IGNORANCE IS BLISS, and I was plenty blissful watching Carol and Niji go through the various games Terrie had taught us. I'm a very hands-on person, though, and before long I couldn't resist getting on the end of the lead rope opposite Niji, with Carol looking on, trying to give me pointers. When I got the responses I was looking for, it was one of the most exhilarating experiences ever for me. Communication with a horse was addictive—even with all the fumbling rope-management issues, I could stay and work on it all day (I still can). The breakthroughs in understanding fascinated me, and when it started to work for me and Niji, it was just awesome. When things fell apart though, which was all the time for me back then, I not only got frustrated, but became petrified that I'd messed up Carol's horse.

Carol taught me all about horse care basics. When Niji came home, we immediately got him on track with regular worming, a farrier, and feed. Then Terrie and Bev lent Carol some books and videos, and together we began learning about this natural horsemanship stuff. The videos were from a variety of clinicians, but mostly Pat and Linda Parelli—not only of the precisely edited, step-by-step kind, but also of some actual clinics in process, with all their unplanned situations, which I particularly like. These videos began to pile up around the house, and the Parellis' entertaining, yet didactic, stories began to sink into our consciousness.

Clinician Pat Parelli is the source of the "Seven Games." He and his wife Linda Parelli have a simple and fun way figured out for people to get started with their horses on the right foot. Even if human and horse have endured a long and tough relationship for some time, usually things can improve between them almost immediately once the human opens to a new understanding and sets about things a little differently.

Before long, Carol traveled with Bev, Terrie, and some other local horse folk down to North Carolina to see Pat and Linda Parelli in action at one of their clinics. She came home even more excited about natural horsemanship. She told stories about such feats as Pat getting his horse in perfect synch with his steps, including quick stops and backing up, and even getting him to lie down. She spoke about how Pat and Linda had used a big ball, a tarp, and barrels to play their games in various ways. Most impressive to Carol was the way the horses were around them—relaxed and so completely willing. This only redoubled our interest, and things with Niji improved all the while.

Several points unfold as one travels deeper into this kind of horsemanship. Early on I realized that a great deal of what is happening with natural horsemanship as a movement is the creation of a language. It may be that as a writer I'm particularly aware of the language usage. However, anyone can see how specific terms are coming into broad acceptance within natural horsemanship circles (and beyond), and that these are key to folks sharing an understanding of this gentler way with horses. Basically, a new way of talking is evolving to help get this way of being with horses across to people.

I'm certain many brilliant horsemen and women over the centuries have discovered these means of better communicating with horses. Dr. Robert M. Miller and Rick Lamb have devoted a section of their book, *The Revolution in Horsemanship*, to the evolution of natural horsemanship, which on their timeline starts with Xenophon, a Greek horseman who lived around 400 BC, and progresses through the ages. What is happening now, in part, is that some capable cowboys have found a way to talk about and teach some of this Better Way with horses to others. In essence, there now exists a clear road map decent enough for large numbers of people to find that destination. If you read up on natural horsemanship, or watch the available videos, you begin to come across words like: lateral flexion, disengage, untrack, soft feel, release, pressure, timing, groundwork, and such. These have combined to create a dictionary of vocabulary specific to this Better Way with horses.

The single most striking and important point I learned early on wasn't an exercise or a cue or what tack works best, but rather a philosophy. If you boil down all the natural horsemanship hubbub, you reach the fact that the very foundation of natural horsemanship is an *understanding*. The core of getting better with horses is considering our relationship to them and understanding the position of humans and horses in the evolutionary scheme of things. Stated simply, humans are the ultimate predators and horses the ultimate prey animals. There never has been a more capable predator than the human, with his thumb, big brain, and ability to create technology to find and kill anything and everything. Likewise, every cell of the horse is designed to recognize danger at a distance and make lightning-fast tracks in the opposite direction from it in a nanosecond. It's like a salmon deciding to trust a bear, relax in his grip, and decide it's a dandy idea to go swimming together. The amazing thing is that horses, miraculously, can overcome this hardwiring and work with people. It is probably the only thing that saved them from going the way of the buffalo.

The next step is to put this understanding to use. If we hold in mind the fact that horses are flight machines and we are potentially their worst nightmare, if we "see things from the horse's point of view," as clinician Harry Whitney puts it, we can begin to form a relationship of understanding with them, rather than the more traditional one of domination. The horse cannot grasp what it must be like to be a predator, so it's up to us to use that big brain we're blessed with for a positive endeavor and consider how things are for the prey animal and adapt.

Humans even can take it a step further and observe how horses interact among themselves and try to mimic the means of

Seeing eye-to-eye with Niji.

communication they use in their herds. This is how the term "natural horsemanship" came about—that we as humans try to communicate with horses using the ways they naturally talk to each other in a herd situation. Parelli explains his usage of the phrase in the opening to his book *Natural Horse*Man*Ship*. He says "natural" in this usage is synonymous with "native, instinctive, inborn, inherent, and intuitive." He puts forth the idea that people can adopt a way of communicating with horses that allows people to communicate in a positive, safe, gentle way, as opposed to using mechanics, fear, and intimidation, which is the way many "normal" humans approach interaction with horses. Monty Roberts offers a similar argument, calling the natural language of horses that can be observed and used by humans "Equus."

The talk horses use isn't vocal, like human language, but is a system of postures and often even the most subtle looks. The slightest twitch of an ear will not go unnoticed by other horses. Some people—Tom Dorrance in particular is credited with this fantastic ability—came to understand how people can interpret this horse talk and put it to use. This is the basis of the Better Way with horses.

A whole host of other stuff came along with discovering natural horsemanship. As I broadened my search for information, I became exposed to an increasing number of clinicians and, therefore, more and more ways of doing things with horses (some of them conflicting!). I found using a rope halter and long lead line helpful. I tried a carrot stick with a string on the end, but gave that up after awhile, finding that things with our horses went just as well, and sometimes better, without it. You can get as much gear as your wallet and tack room can handle, but I've found what works for me doesn't take much—typically that single rope halter and lead rope, or a bridle with an egg butt snaffle bit and mecate-type reins, depending on what we're up to. And that's it for me, other than a saddle and a couple of blankets, and maybe tying a plastic bag on the end of a rod once in awhile to use as a flag for a few situations. But all horses and all people are different, and I'm sure different techniques and different gear suit a variety of situations. Plus, I'm still learning, so it's entirely possible I might feel differently in the future about this.

This brings out another point that just amazed me early on. Nowhere else have I seen English and Western riders commingling except at natural horsemanship clinics. The natural horsemanship movement is a melting pot—it is the United States of horsemanship, with people from every discipline coming together. How bizarre, I thought, the first time I saw an English rider watching intently and learning from a cowboy complete with chaps and cowboy hat! Talk about busting through cultural barriers. That alone is proof that this way with horses is largely about the *relationship* between horse and human, and a person's chosen discipline makes no difference.

To be honest, working with Niji improved my life in many ways. With horses, I learned, you cannot appear aggressive; that only makes for a bad situation. If you think about how the horse views you, Super Predator, it becomes obvious that if you are trying to gain the horse's trust and confidence, getting angry and becoming a maniac in his presence will only justify what his genes are telling him—that you are going to eat him! And horses don't forget things. This pretty much freaked me out at first, and I worried over everything I did when around Niji. But, it's true that you might have a hundred hours of great, positive moments with your horse, but get angry one time and hit that horse or act foolish with him, and you may never again enjoy a close relationship with him. What I'm getting at is that I learned patience. I thought five kids taught me patience—but no, not enough, although I think working with horses and working with children is a great analogy. We truly get back from them what we put into them. Niji at times pushed the patience envelope for me, and I found the strength to walk away sometimes. It was quite a lesson for me to learn how compulsive I am about accomplishing tasks. I tend to work at something obsessively until I get it done, and try to be quick about it. With horses—much, much to my personal difficulty, and going completely against my deeply entrenched work ethic—at times the best thing to do is *nothing*. Wow, that's hard for me.

Horses, it seems from my experience discovering natural horsemanship, are mirrors. At first, I only saw the most obvious differences in horses. I could see a horse that limped, I could see one that danced around its handler nonstop, or one that bucked with a saddle on its back. Now, with some time working with horses under my belt, I can see more subtle aspects of a horse's posture, like how he holds his head, or if he licks and chews. These are things that have been pointed out to me along the way by many different people sharing what they have learned, trying to get better with horses in a gentle way. But, it seems, the horse's condition is always a reflection of how the human or humans in his life have treated him. I have learned as much about what I'm doing wrong from horses developing new problems than any other single indicator. Short of a physical problem, if your horse starts doing something new and unfavorable, take a close look at yourself. What a tough lesson for us humans! But what better one could we learn? This is a major part of discovering natural horsemanship.

It isn't surprising that many (if not an absolute majority of) people discover natural horsemanship because *their horses* have problems. He won't load in a trailer. He won't stand still for me to get on. He won't let me catch him and put a halter on him. Then, when they get help for such issues with a good clinician of the Better Way and come out the other side with the improvements they sought in their horses, it is the *people* who have been retrained, and the horses' improvements are only the by-product of those improved humans.

Natural horsemanship is fun and rewarding, but it's incredibly tough too. The personal growth required from the handler in order to improve with horses makes it so challenging. One need only read through Buck Brannaman's book *Believe* to get a sense of this. The book is an anthology of personal stories written by people who have undergone major life transformations that trace back to work with horses at Buck's clinics. The chapters have titles like, "Coping with Fear," "Working Things Through," and "Believing in Yourself," and for good reason.

Once I began to feel pretty good about a few groundwork exercises with Niji, another horse came into my world, bringing a whole new set of challenges. The beginnings of this new relationship would show me that horses are just as different from one another as people. And you can't use what you learn with one as a cookie cutter, sure-fire method for all the rest. The odyssey has been one challenge after another right from the beginning, but that's where the growth for me has taken place. Working through those challenges, overcoming fears, and getting dirty is where the fulfillment of it originates. If you can get the core understanding of natural horsemanship down, then you can start freely using different approaches with each horse to get through to his mind in each particular situation.

You begin to develop a tool chest of sorts, where you can go rummage around and pick out a way you've been taught that is just what you need for a job, or maybe combine a few things together to develop something you haven't been shown verbatim, but that works in your situation.

Discovering natural horsemanship is more profound than just discovering natural horsemanship. It alters the balance of one's life, tipping it in a favorable direction. I have found it to be so already, and I'm just getting started.

CHAPTER THREE

NAMING MY TWO

SELF-AWARENESS OF MY IGNORANCE about horses agitated me as I started trying to get better with Niji. Honestly, at this stage I knew more about playing seven games with horses than about seven colors horses can be. I hadn't even put a saddle on a horse seven times, for that matter. Attempting conversation with knowledgeable horse folk made me feel like an idiot. Equally trying was that I was not equipped to discern who was and who was not a knowledgeable horse person in order to realize when I really *should* feel like an idiot. Niji, living here now, made hands-on experience with one mellow gelding easy enough, but I started to hunger to know more about other types of horses and horse activities. The draw to horses in general had me in its clutches; it was just a question of what type of horse might be best for me. I was really starting from ground zero, and other than having a pretty good idea that Quarter Horses must be well suited for cattle work, and Budweiser had a fine team of Clydesdales, zero is what I knew about horses.

It was early fall by this point, and Niji's modest accommodations near the house were in good shape. The paddock's boundary was defined with permanent woven wire fencing and two large galvanized gates. The area within included some flat southern-facing spots where the sun hit most of the day and a bit of wooded hillside to explore. Through either gate, additional small flat areas defined by temporary electric fencing could be opened up for rotation to provide some supplementary grazing. A small run-in shed built from poles cut near the site, sided with rough sawn lumber and roofed in tin, completed Niji's new home.

The farm has a pretty nice small field on another higher ridge about a half mile away as well. We had planted potatoes and corn in it for several years, but the spring before Niji came home, we sowed it in an orchard grass/white clover mixture, thinking to prepare for a couple of cows in the not-too-distant future. I fenced that field in with a quick two-strand electric fence to give Niji more grazing space and a pasture with more room to move around in. It also provided the additional room to accommodate a horse for myself in the future, probably sometime in the spring. Niji could use the equine companionship, even though he and Sancho, an older Alpine goat with full set of curved horns, had an entertaining relationship. Plus, the gelding had truly connected with Carol rather than me, so as obsessed as I was becoming with horses, it was only right I get my own.

At this point, I started looking at ads in the local papers and the regional horse trader magazines with color photos, not as a serious search for a horse, but rather to educate myself on horses in general and see just what was available around here and what prices were like. Whenever an interesting horse was listed for sale close by, I called and asked questions about it. I'd even get Carol to go for a ride and have a look with me occasionally. I figured learning by just going to see horses for sale was a fine idea, even though it wasn't time financially, psychologically, or seasonally, with winter coming, to actually buy one at this point. I made this clear on the phone with folks before going to see them, being honest and up-front so they would understand I wasn't a serious buyer, just a window shopper, and not waste time with me if they didn't want to.

Before long, an ad for Paso Finos with our local telephone exchange was listed in the newspaper classifieds. I called and learned that the horses were just up the road a few miles. Carol agreed to go have a look with me, so I arranged it with the woman on the phone, and the next morning we drove over.

In a steep pasture with a creek and two enormous oaks between a house at the top of a hill and a road at the bottom was a herd of seven horses. Carol had been telling me about Paso Finos on the way over. She reminded me we'd seen a video of them at a show—small boned, refined, and with a most peculiar gait—their feet seem to move in a blur of speed, yet the animal travels very slowly. It reminded me of the Road Runner when he's gearing up to take off as Coyote starts to chase him. In the taped show, the horses carried their riders along a plank that must have been rigged with a microphone. As they crossed the plank the hooves tapped out a cadence like a military snare drum: rat, tat, tat, tat. Carol also mentioned they have tiny feet compared to most other breeds.

The owner, a short, squat woman with chaotic frizzy hair, came out and greeted us. Carol pointed out a buckskin to educate me on yet another horse color and marking pattern. My study of the herd revealed big feet and none of the gait I'd seen in that video. Within five minutes of being around these horses, Carol and I exchanged glances that confirmed my suspicion that these didn't seem to be Paso Finos. I was relieved to finally know enough to distinguish when someone else was clueless.

Which brings up an important lesson I learned that day— you need to be certain, when looking into buying a horse or seeking sound advice on training, that the people you deal with are honest and know what they're talking about. It is a hard thing to discern when you are a novice yourself. You may need to be quite cautious until you find people you are certain are capable hands with horses. This woman didn't mean any harm, but she knew very little about horses—and she had no idea truly how little, which I think made her dangerous. At the same time, she was quick to try to convince us of what she believed about her horses' breeding and quality of training, even though it contradicted reality. The rest of the events of that morning were amusing in a way, but also disturbing. The woman insisted on showing us why Paso Finos are so great—that their gait is the smoothest in the world and once you try one you'll never go back. She managed with considerable difficulty (and a bucket of grain) to get a halter on her main saddle horse, while getting mugged for the grain. Carol and I held back the herd as she led that horse through the gate, quite a feat even with all three of us. By the garage, she saddled him up, then led the gelding into a round pen set up behind the house. She had barely stepped up into the saddle, thrown her leg over his back, and gathered the reins before he took off with her and started running circles, waving his head around. I couldn't help but notice, after having seen the ABCs of natural horsemanship explained on video multiple times, the obvious lack of groundwork before climbing on the horse. She said something about using methods from a video as she whipped past us, bouncing in the saddle so hard I really wondered about her earlier comment on the smooth Paso Fino gait.

After a few minutes of what I might call trot-near-gallop, and with the horse becoming increasingly wild as the reins stayed taut in his mouth, she called to us, "Go ahead and open the gate!"

Carol and I exchanged looks again and paused, both wondering if that was really the best idea. Then I opened the gate. The way that horse shot out of the round pen, Carol and I jumping out of the way in either direction, was like a combination of the starting gate at the racetrack and the bucking chute at the rodeo.

The woman continued to try to talk about the soft Paso gait while her backside slapped so hard against her saddle that the words came out staccato—I felt sorry for her kidneys. She trotted back and forth, back and forth, and back and forth between where we stood and a fence a couple hundred feet away. She was unable to keep the horse still for more than two words when she came up to us before she was off to the races again. Ten minutes later, when she managed to get the horse back into the round pen and dismounted, she asked me, "Do you want to ride him?"

I declined—I might have been real green, but knew better than to accept that offer! Carol asked what was now a rhetorical question: "So . . . do these Paso Finos have papers?"

"Well, no," came the response.

As quickly and tactfully as we could, we climbed into our escape vehicle and fled the scene. All the way home we mused at the bizarre episode we had just witnessed, with the discussion swinging from extreme amusement to extreme concern.

This experience illustrates some important points. The main one is that the woman never considered the horse's behavior to be a problem. To her, that ride was perfectly normal. She was obviously quite fearless on her horse, a trait I thought I could use a little more of, but in this situation it was absolutely dangerous. Her relationship with the horse was far from smooth or calm. The situation drove home for me the point that people don't always use good judgment around horses, can be in denial about the condition of their relationship with their horses, and might nevertheless be quick to share their opinions as if they were authorities.

I also realized that if I hadn't known better, I might have climbed on that horse for a ride and gotten hurt—or been convinced that those horses were Paso Finos. I might even have purchased one and tried to go trail riding right off the bat, since they were supposed to be "broke." It is not hard to find people with years of "experience" with horses who know very little about them. There is no shortage of self-proclaimed trainers, breeders, and professionals out there. You have to arm yourself with knowledge and good judgment to avoid catastrophe sometimes.

A few weeks after the Paso Fino incident, a black, sixteen-hand Tennessee Walking Horse gelding advertised in a horse trading magazine caught my eye. At the time, I thought a tall horse would suit me, and I was particularly interested in horses that were sixteen hands or better. The same phone number was listed under the picture of several other horses as well, so I called, figuring it would be a great place to see a range of horses for sale at once. The seller turned out to be a local farmer whose main operation was beef cattle, but who also rode and traded horses and always had a dozen or two coming and going. I gathered up Carol and our nine-year-old granddaughter Xantha, who was staying with us at the time, and we went to check the gelding out.

The horse was already saddled upon our arrival and was hanging out calmly, tied to a hitching rail. I warned the farmer of my extreme noviceness. "My kids ride this horse," he answered confidently. "I don't bring a horse home they can't ride." With this, he called over one of his equally confident preteen boys, who climbed up onto the tall, thin Walking Horse, gathered up the reins, and took off like Dale Earnhardt. The youngster leaned back in the Western saddle and loped near the barn. After a few laps, figure eights, and whatever else the boy had in his repertoire of fancy moves, he brought the horse around to a stop next to me, hopped down, handed me the reins, and then went to find another race car to burn rubber in.

"Uh, okay . . . " I said, nervous but figuring if I kept the horse slow and steered fairly well I'd be safe in the area by the barn. No sooner did I throw my leg over the horse and take hold of the reins than the horse took off. I pulled back and tried to stop, but that horse did whatever it wanted to. I didn't even have the one-rein stop at my disposal, I was so inexperienced at this point. We tore this way across the yard and that way down the driveway and then back up and onto a pile of gravel where the gelding managed a pirouette before stopping at the summit momentarily. Then he was off again, back down the gravel pile and across behind the barn. Somehow we got more or less stopped back near the hitching rail, and I managed to get off alive. I was shaking. I could barely stand up. I handed the reins back to the man, speechless, with a dumb look on my face. Obviously surprised—although most likely at my inability in the saddle—he said, "Well . . . uh, guess we'll have to take a closer look at this horse. I can't believe he did that."

Whatever, I thought, just happy to be on dry land again, and I then looked over to see Xantha—who had never been on a horse before—riding around just fine on a palomino Quarter Horse mare, smiling from ear to ear. She was nine and doing a whole lot better than me at thirty-five. Since I wasn't seriously looking for a horse anyway, and I had warned him I was a total beginner, I figured that no harm was done. I could go home, lick my wounds, work harder with Niji, and venture out again into the world sometime in a year or two or three to look at other horses. Then it happened.

"Let me show you a horse," the farmer said.

"That's all right," I replied, "I'm not really ready to buy anyway, like I said."

"She's right here. This is a horse that we give to all the people who *can't* ride when we go on trail rides," he reported. A young woman, about college age, overheard our discussion and spoke up. "Oh, she's *wonderful*. She actually taught me how to ride."

And there she was, tied to a gate. A quiet, bay Tennessee Walking Horse mare. At that time, with coarse hair and withdrawn eyes, she didn't stand out in the crowd of taller, flashier, more energetic horses. She was like the quiet, invisible girl at school with her good grades, regular clothes, and few friends. But, like that girl, when brought to one's attention, it was evident how beautiful she really was—and that a deep soul had been there all along.

Meeting this horse was one of the strangest events in my life. It was like she recognized me from some other place and time.

And there she was.

The farmer insisted on saddling her up—I think he felt bad about the near-death experience on the other horse, which wasn't the horse's fault. Something about her look even gave me the courage to go ahead and climb into the saddle and ride around after the other wicked ordeal. She took good care of me, and I managed to have a good time just walking her here and there—*slowly*. He offered her for sale, for much more money than I had at the time, but a fair price nonetheless. Also, she was supposed to be bred, so it was a two-for-one deal. I thanked him anyway, restated my present position, and went home.

After meeting that horse, I was a complete wreck. I couldn't sleep. All I could think about was that bay mare. When I finally did fall asleep, I dreamed about her that night and woke up even more nervous and nutty the next day. I could not stop thinking about her and was actually quite neurotic about it. It was near my birthday, so when my father called mid-morning and I talked on and on about her, he offered to put some money towards her as an early present. I went up to the farm to see if perhaps a layaway plan could be worked out. The farmer loaded her up right then, and she came home to my upper field that afternoon.

The whole whirlwind of events sent me spiraling. Something about this horse really grabbed me at a deep level. Twenty-four hours before, I was just curious enough to go check out some sale horses up close for educational purposes; now I had one—and most probably two—right here at home! *Unbelievable*, I thought over and over.

The mare unloaded very matter-of-factly off the stock trailer and led easily into the upper pasture and started grazing contently. She had "more whoa than go," as is sometimes said of a more sedentary horse. No high-performance engine was fine with me at that point. She was young, though, only three, and pregnant. Her history was pretty sketchy too, so I was uncertain just what quality of feed or care she had been provided before coming to the place where I had purchased her.

Carol brought Niji up from the other paddock for introductions, and the two horses romped around for awhile, tails flagged, the mare showing off her Walking Horse gait. She proved right then she could move when she wanted to. I was absolutely enchanted when she moved in that exaggerated trot. Somehow, it felt, she had chosen me as her person rather than me choosing her as my horse.

So now that we were getting acquainted and she had suddenly moved in, she needed a name.

Naming the horse was a serious business for me. In general, I feel it can't be done before the arrival of a horse. It is a collaborative effort, an interactive process, the horse participating fully, sharing personality, looks, opinions, and ideas.

Of course, some danger looms in allowing any animal to help with the naming process. Some years ago we had a litter of Rhodesian Ridgeback/English Mastiff cross puppies, and the sickly runt, not more than a handful at the time, won Carol's heart. She carried the brindle fur ball around in one hand, nursing him along and calling him "my little Teeney Weeney," which stuck like chewing gum to the bottom of a sneaker. Now there is a 155-pound Teeney Weeney running around the farm. Introducing him to new people always gets a laugh.

The problem really isn't finding an appropriate name for an animal—one will surface sooner or later, to be sure—but the time that it can take to come up with it. Carol was fortunate that Niji came pre-named. Plus, he happens to be one of the friendliest horses around, so Niji being Ojibwa for "friend" is perfect.

No real name had traveled with the bay mare from her former life. The Earnhardt kids on the farm we bought her from called her Blaze. That was just too common and generic, and she really has more of a stripe than a blaze—not to mention that she hardly had a blazing personality—so Blaze was out and the search began. Another Native American word that described her in some way might be a nice match alongside Niji, I thought, but even after hours combing various books and conducting Internet searches, nothing that felt right appeared.

As days turned to weeks, the family began to turn up the heat on me. You wouldn't think it really affected any of the five kids, all of whom live out in the world now, but it apparently bothered them. Even our granddaughter began to rib me hard. As weeks stretched into more than a month, they even began to mutiny and call her "Poops-on-the-ground" and other equally horrid things. I thought about Teeney Weeney and figured I'd better do *something* before she accidentally got stuck with "Poops"—or worse!

Still, naming the mare was too important to just throw in the towel and go with whatever. Then again, trying to do ground-work and saying, "Great job, You. Come here, Whoever-you-are," gets old.

Finally, a break came. Helena Halmari, a Finnish friend and linguist who helps me with occasional writing in the world of Finnish literature, sent some suggestions from her native tongue. We had corresponded a few times about my horse nam-ing dilemma, and I had described the mare's sweet nature to her. Helena volunteered a list of Finnish potentials, among them "Sokeri," the Finnish word for "sugar." She explained that using this noun for an animal's name wasn't common, but still would work in Finnish. As far as I was concerned, it was perfect. It was atypical, had a great ring to it—not too many words end in "i" and we had two of them, Niji and Sokeri—and she is awfully sweet. The pronunciation is a little tricky, especially the correct Finnish one, which places the emphasis on the first syllable and rolls the "r" a bit like German, but I loved it. It wasn't long before the name changed in general usage to Soke (pronounced So-kay), or often just So. It seems perfect for her.

So, that problem was solved to the relief of all, including me. But of course another cropped up to replace it. I had been warned of Sokeri's early breeding, and the one shed in the paddock by the house wasn't sufficiently large for foaling. Through November and December, despite snow and near-zero temperatures and quite a bit of wind that year, I began framing up a new shed at the edge of the upper pasture. I made it 14 x 16 feet to accommodate foaling needs. The area around the pasture is full of hardwood trees, so a great deal of excellent, straight hardwood pole material was at hand, which was put to use as framing material, and before long, the shell of the shed was up. I knocked along on nailing up the siding, misappropriating some white pine lumber that had been earmarked for another project, and Ken came in for several days and helped me in single-digit temperatures to get the tin roof on. By January, as Sokeri began looking more and more like a big pear with four legs and a tail, the structure was complete.

New buildings are obviously more exciting for humans. After all the push to get the thing built quickly, Sokeri wouldn't go in it at first, especially when the weather was bad and it seemed to be the best time to be inside, away from the elements. It was a reminder—another lesson—that these were *horses*. They spook easily, especially in confined spaces. They are hardwired to keep a clear line of sight around them for predators and hate spooky noises, especially if they cannot see them. This all added up to Sokeri staying clear of that shed.

I started feeding her in there and leaving Niji in the upper pasture with her as well. Niji prefers a shed in bad weather for the most part, and the mare seemed to frequent the structure more as he hung out in it quite a bit. January slipped into February, her udder began to swell, and before long she began to stand with a most miserable look on her face, or even lay down flat on her side, *in the shed*!

I figured she had to foal soon, so we moved Niji back over to the house paddock, and then she seemed to go back the other way and become more comfortable again. A week went by, then two, and I figured without any real change we probably weren't on the verge of a foal after all.

Every horse person I spoke with about foaling warned that mares always foal in the middle of the night. Never when anyone is around, and usually when the weather is just horrible. We had just been through plenty of bad weather, but then in late February, it broke. The sun came out and the temperatures soared to the mid-fifties. I still kept a close eye on her. On the 25th of February, it was really nice outside. I fed Sokeri breakfast in the shed as usual. She showed no signs of being anything but perfectly content. I went about my morning and then decided at about eleven o'clock to go get a load of gravel for a spot in the road that was getting pretty bad. I almost just passed the shed without stopping in for a visit, but I couldn't resist petting Soke. I parked the truck, got out, and headed over.

Approaching the shed along a path through the woods from the road, I saw Sokeri stick her head out to check on the noise of my steps. She had a wild look in her eye, but that wasn't unusual when I came up this way, where she couldn't see me approaching. But this was kind of a different look . . . more of a panicked nervousness.

"Hey So, what ya doing?" I asked and stroked her head. Then I stepped between the two strands of electric fence. When I looked at her strange bug-eyed expression again, I took another step and peeked into the shed. There, standing, still wet, peeking right back at me from behind its mother, was a bright-eyed, tannish-colored foal.

It caught me totally off guard. I was stunned! I guess between the weather, time of day, and her normal feeding a few hours before it never occurred to me that this could be the day. The mare let me into the shed without a problem, and the foal stood on long

The new foal had arrived.

spindly legs as I slowly went right up to him and began softly rubbing him. No fear was present in him whatsoever. I checked—it was a colt. I ran to the truck, sped to the house, and got Carol. Abandoning the gravel idea, I spent the rest of the day alternating between giving mother and foal time alone and getting some time in with them myself to be a part of this incredible first day.

And then the whole naming scenario started over again. A week went by, and the family was on my case fast and furious this time. I was adamant: "He has to be alive long enough for me to figure out just *who* he is." Luckily, it didn't take long for him to let us know his name. He was being called by name before I even realized it was his name: Whipper Snapper, a perfect fit. It wouldn't be long before his whipping and snapping would bring about a serious and unfortunate set of circumstances, but for the first weeks, the colt was perfect and the joy around here profound.

CHAPTER FOUR

WHIPPER TEARS HIS EYE

ONE EVENING SIX WEEKS AFTER discovering the foal with Sokeri in the shed, I was standing beside mare and foal in that very same spot, when Whipper Snapper, without warning, sprang forward and ran straight into the wall of the shed. To this day I don't know what got into the little colt.

Daily, I had been working on teaching him to pick up his feet by touching the chestnuts in the front and hocks in the back. He would step backwards with a soft touch to his chest. I had been getting him accustomed to having a halter around his face and even had one on him several times. Everything was going better than I could have hoped. But that day as I put down his evening feed and he started eating, as did his mother farther in the shed behind us, he just sprang ahead and smacked into the shed wall. Perhaps he was startled, cued by his mother, or simply felt like kicking up his heels. Perhaps I did something to worry him, although I did nothing different from every other feeding that week, and I was standing right beside him when he bolted.

Whip had bumped into the walls before, as most foals do on occasion, so I wasn't alarmed at first. But then he began shaking his head repeatedly. "Did you knock yourself silly?" I said out loud as I stepped toward him to take a closer look. I noticed moisture around his right eye. I got in close and saw a tear, nearly a half-inch long, in his eyeball. Fluid was draining from the globe, and a flap of torn eye tissue was hanging loose.

That moment of realization will forever haunt me—I ran to my truck and tore up the farm road to the house. I got our large animal veterinarian, Thomas Bibb, DVM, on the phone right away. Not one to panic, he asked me to go back to the shed to make certain I had seen a tear on the eye rather than a splinter of some kind. I was certain, but I went back and took Carol with me to confirm what I had seen.

When I called back with the news, Bibb did not hesitate. "Get the mare and foal to Tech [the Virginia-Maryland Regional Veterinary Hospital in Blacksburg, Virginia] as soon as possible," he said, adding that he would call ahead so the hospital would be prepared for our arrival.

Carol and I quickly brainstormed on whom to borrow a trailer from. First we tried Bev, but got her machine and left a message. Then I tried a farrier friend who lived close by, got his voicemail, and left a message. Knowing Whipper was up there in that condition made sitting still making calls excruciating. Luckily the phone rang back almost immediately, saving me from losing my mind, and in a flurry of calls between us and a few folks, I lined up the farrier's two-horse trailer for the trip. I went straight to the truck, which was on empty, made it to the farm supply store just as the clerk was locking the door, talked him into turning the pump back on, got some gas, fetched the trailer, and sped back to the house in record time.

As often happens in times of crisis, the subsequent series of events following the disaster were blessedly free of complications. Whipper was still nursing, so Sokeri would have to go as well. Sokeri loaded easily for the trip to the hospital, as did Whipper Snapper, who never had been in a trailer before. Although by now it was cold and dark, the ride to the clinic was swift and uneventful. The hospital was not busy that evening, so the staff was able to get right to Whipper. Within an hour and a half of the injury, the colt was getting care, and the mare, standing close by, was calm and cooperative.

Surgical Resident Graham Keys, DVM, took charge of Whipper's case. After an initial examination, he spoke plainly about the damage to the eye. It was significant. Whipper had sliced through the full thickness of the cornea, the clear outer covering of the eye, and the iris, the colored muscular structure underneath, was poking through the wound opening. Although Keys did not say it, it was obvious that Whipper's eye was in jeopardy.

At this point, Keys called in Marc Rainbow, DVM, an ophthalmology resident. With Whipper sedated and his eyelid numbed, Rainbow examined the eye with an ophthalmoscope to determine the extent of the damage. The two surgeons conferred and decided that the length of the tear was on the threshold of being irreparable—it was unlikely that vision could be restored. If the eye was simply removed, however, Whipper's developing skull would lose an important anatomical "landmark," which meant it might grow asymmetrically.

On the plus side, we had been quick to get Whipper to the hospital. The injury was still fresh and relatively clean, so infection was less likely to set in if we did choose to have the eye repaired.

My nerves were shot. My mouth was a dry, barren desert. The sum total of the past two hours brought me to a state of strange peace at this point. I guess I had accepted the situation. I knew Carol and I had done all we could, and now it was handed over to those who were best suited to help the colt.

Still, Carol and I faced a huge decision—should we agree to surgery to try to save the eye or simply have it removed? It wasn't a hard decision, though—I was more worried about Whipper's general health than about the sight in his injured eye. Already my experience with the type of horsemanship we were pursuing made me confident we could work around the blindness on one side, but if the colt ended up with a facial asymmetry that interfered with his bite and chewing, his health could be compromised for the rest of his life. We gave the go-ahead for the repair, assured that the eye could be removed later anyway if need be.

We left the fluorescent light of the hospital, where time had melted away, and walked outside where we were reminded by the cold and black star-filled sky that it was nighttime. The trailer faced us, doors still open. I closed them up, checked the hitch, and we headed back through Blacksburg and onto the winding mountain roads of Floyd County towards the Blue

Ridge Parkway. We were nearly halfway home when we passed a car that turned around behind us and approached us with blue lights flashing. The trailer lights weren't working and the trailer had no tags, but the officer was sympathetic to our predicament, and with hazard flashers blinking, we made our way the rest of the way home.

At 4 a.m. the next morning, as promised, we received a call from the vet hospital. Surgery was complete; mare and foal had been reunited in a recovery stall. It was only later, when Keys explained to us the complex two-hour surgery, that we came to appreciate all that had been done for our colt that night.

Whipper Snapper had sustained a traumatic corneal perforation, Keys explained. A sharp object—possibly a small splinter from the shed wall—had lacerated the cornea exposing the interior of the eye. The outer wall of the eye is normally under some pressure from the fluid within. The laceration allowed fluid to escape, decreasing pressure and pushing the iris forward so that it protruded through the perforation almost instantly.

During surgery, Rainbow injected fluid back into the eye to restore ocular pressure—essentially "reinflating" the eye and returning the iris to its normal position. He also performed a keratectomy, removing the damaged portions of cornea at the margins of the perforation. The "clean" edges were then sutured closed with filament finer than a human hair.

Next the surgeon created a conjunctival pedicle graft, securing a flap of the blood-vessel rich conjunctiva over the injury site. Besides serving as a protective covering, the graft aids healing by increasing blood supply and nutrition to the wound area. Over time, we were told, the cornea would absorb the graft and only a minor scar would remain.

Thanks to the surgical talents of Rainbow, Whipper's eye was repaired, but its condition was delicate at best.

Whipper Snapper and Sokeri spent the next three days in the hospital. During that time, I learned how to administer medication through the sub-palpebral lavage catheter that had been placed in Whipper's eyelid during surgery. The catheter was attached to a narrow tube that passed through the upper eyelid up to the poll and along the crest of the neck, where it was affixed to the mane. A syringe was used to push medications through the tube to the catheter and onto the eye. Designed to facilitate frequent delivery of medication to painful eyes, this lavage system was a godsend for our fidgety foal, who wouldn't stand still for having his eyelids pried open several times a day.

At home, I got an intensive four-week lesson in horseology, as Whipper and Sokeri spent nearly a month in the shed, now converted into an enclosed stall. Four times a day, we used the lavage system to deliver a variety of drugs to Whipper's eye. To ward off infection, he received an antibiotic cream and an antifungal solution, and to promote healing, we administered serum taken from the colt's own blood. We also gave him atropine, which dilated the iris and kept it from adhering to the cornea, a painful complication called synechia.

In addition, Whipper received oral antibiotics and Banamine, for inflammation and pain, daily. He wore a halter with a protective hood that incorporated a plastic cup to cover his injured eye. For each medication session, this apparatus had to be removed, so Carol and I teamed up—me holding the colt and she administering meds and removing, sterilizing, and replacing the eye cup and hood. Whipper's small size, regular handling, and easygoing demeanor made all of this much easier than it might otherwise have been. I worked continually to get better with my feel, giving Whipper release from the pressure of holding him, and praising him with soft strokes when he'd stand still for the procedures. Likewise, I'd try to apply pressure in gradual phases if he needed to be backed or otherwise moved. A couple of times (fewer than you might expect for a young colt cooped up in a fourteen-by-sixteen-foot walled space for a month) we went to the rodeo, and it was all I could do to keep up with him in there and get him settled back down—an absolutely terrifying predicament with his protective eye hood off and lavage tube flying around.

The effort required to maintain the medication schedule, keep the stall cleaned, and ensure that the horses were as happy as possible in their jail cell was more than a full-time job. We gave the first round of medications well before daybreak, then moved on to feeding and mucking. Soon after returning to the house and getting some breakfast, it was time to prepare for the second medication session. The third was done with the evening feeding, and we mucked again afterwards. The final round of medications was given well after dark.

Very little time remained for any regular life—or work for that matter—but we managed this routine for the entire month with the help of a few generous friends.

A week after the horses came home, Dr. Bibb stopped by for a follow-up check on Whipper's eye. He was pleased with the colt's recovery. A few weeks later, he returned to remove the lavage system and declared Whipper well enough to be turned out and start enjoying his youth again, encumbered only by a normal fly mask to give the tender eye some protection and shade from direct sun. We continued to closely monitor the healing of the eye,

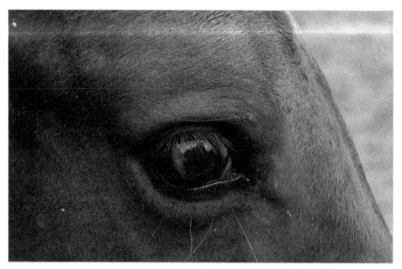

Within months, little evidence remained of the injury.

Whipper and Soke enjoying their freedom.

ready to call Dr. Bibb instantly if anything looked amiss, but each day brought good news and more progress.

Whipper continued to be a lively young colt, and before long, little outward evidence remained of his accident. His face appeared symmetrical as it developed. At first, the eye had substantial whiteness, particularly in the area of the stitches, but this diminished over time. The only residual effect of the injury was a small white line at the side of the eyeball. Having witnessed the immediate aftermath of the injury, I never would have guessed that the eye would ever be as strong and healthy as it became after surgery.

Rudimentary vision tests indicated that Whipper could not see out of his right eye, but Bibb believed that the colt shows some response to bright light on that side. Whatever the case, Whipper seemed to have fully adapted. He wheeled around his pasture like any frisky colt and tagged along freely during trail rides, with that carefree confidence that comes with youth and good health.

CHAPTER FIVE

FEELING OF A HORSE

THE FIRST THREE DOZEN TIMES I heard natural horse folk say, "You have to *feel of* a horse," I winced and wondered, what in the heck is that supposed to mean? It couldn't be grammatically correct (the writer coming out in me), and I'd never heard anyone talk about "feeling of" something before.

It makes more sense now, this curious word combination. After more than a year of seeking natural horsemanship information like a person with his hair on fire seeks water, I've even come to be grateful for this phrasing curiosity.

As far as I can tell, "to feel of a horse" is a Dorranceism. That is, a term coined by and unique to the Dorrance brothers, Bill and

Tom, the men who are credited as the founders of natural horse-manship. The beauty in this odd, potentially grammatically in-correct statement is that it has a singular usage. It completely belongs to natural horsemanship and has a particular meaning.

Which leads to the crux of the matter: what *does* it mean? Well, that's a whole other thing . . . .

I can tell you that feeling of a horse and a horse feeling of you are *the* goals of natural horsemanship. Once those are in place, the relationship is automatic. Horse and rider are as one. There can come a state where you need only to think what you'd like to do with your horse next and the horse is doing it before you even move a rein or shift your weight. I've heard this is true; I'm prob-ably a million hours on a horse away from it myself. Feeling of a horse is the invisible connection and communication that can exist between horse and human, and apparently explaining it is nearly impossible. If you've ever read Tom Dorrance's book, *True Unity*, you know what I mean. Here's an example from page 23:

> When I am trying to put it [the ability to figure things out with a horse, a.k.a. *feel*] into words and am right there where the horse can respond, and the person doesn't get it, it's pretty hard to think of words that will take care of it in a book.

Natural horsemanship is so much like a spiritual quest that it likely is one. In fact, feeling of a horse is like enlightenment, in that it's totally nebulous. You can't be told how to find it exactly, and even *what* it is defies definition.

As with any such quest, some of the basics you first work on can result in profound and quick change and improvement in areas of your life. Being honest, for instance, has the power to drastically help out a person who has lacked that quality before. Likewise, understanding about the proper application and release of pressure with horses can change your relationship with them for the better in ten minutes; it is a cornerstone in the foundation of your quest to get better with horses.

There are quite a few programs out there with books and videos and clinics on practicing meditation, yoga, and such things, just like there are a good number on horsemanship (natural and otherwise) available. But similarly, words fall short of providing the reader the goal in these instances—it must be experienced by the individual to be grasped. If the guru can provide anything, it is likely advice for ways to better be on the lookout for *It*, or a description of how they came across *It*, but there's no way to give the exact steps for each person to go out and find enlightenment or to feel of a horse.

Practicing feel with Niji.

One thing is for sure, and I've experienced this myself; the more time we spend with horses, paying attention to what they have to say to us and each other, and the more time we spend applying what building blocks we can pick up from great horse folk, the more likely we are to catch glimpses of "feel." The more of these glimpses we experience, the more likely we are to put it all together later and be better set up for a real breakthrough at some point.

I've been fortunate to have had some breakthroughs with my mare, Sokeri. Always, with each advance, just as I bask in the sun of my great accomplishment, a new storm cloud of challenge wafts by to block it out. Since each horse is different, feeling of your particular horse becomes necessary for your advancement together.

Sokeri and I have been through this a few times. For example, we made good progress with circling. When I was first able to communicate circling around me in one direction on a lead, stopping to face me, then heading out in the other direction, the delight had me smiling for two days. We both improved with each session. She became lighter on her feet and understood the cues more quickly. I became better at giving the cues and visualizing what I wanted her to do before asking, and got tangled up in the lead rope less frequently. Then, I laid two barrels on their sides at the edge of the round pen in her path to see if she would circle to them and eventually jump. She went up to them, stopped and sniffed. I let her check them out, then sent her the other way back around to them with the same result. When I tried to increase her energy (through what I hoped was *feel*) so she would jump, she fell apart. She would walk over to me even if I tried to send her out, bump into me, or stand pressing against me. If I tried to just circle her like we had been doing just before without the barrels, she still invaded my space and couldn't recoup.

Describing this on the phone to the more advanced natural horse people I know, the response I kept getting was "respect issues." But, inside, I felt that it wasn't about respect. It *felt* not like an attempt to challenge me, or ignore my requests, but rather to seek comfort. The barrels confused her, and she just wanted to be released from the newness of the situation and be close to me.

I concentrated to make certain the cues I sent with my eyes, body, and hands were the same as always, to send her out of my space and get back to circling correctly. As I tried again with the same miserable results, anger flared up in me, and I figured I'd better give it a rest. If she picked up on any feel of mine, anger would be it—not the best message to send when she's already troubled. But I didn't want to send the message that she could fall apart and get release whenever something new came on the scene, either. So I went back to more simple groundwork. And I mean way more simple, like lateral flexion, simple backing up, disengaging her hindquarters, and just rubbing her softly. Then we quit on a good note when she was well in her comfort zone and responding perfectly to the easy stuff.

Perhaps it doesn't matter whether the source of the problem was respect issues or the mare seeking comfort, or even if they might be one and the same—the solution is stepping back, regrouping, and insisting on the desired outcome through pressure and release, approach and retreat. It was, however, important to me that I *felt* what was going on with her. Also, it broadened my experience as relates to feel. I *felt* the flow of understanding between us as she responded, soft, light, and easy, to my requests. I also experienced the opposite and knew from that point onward just what it was like to have her scattered and not responding at all correctly to my requests. If you are spending considerable time with your horse, paying attention to its emotional and mental states, and have a few of the fundamentals of natural horsemanship down, then developing some sense of feel seems to follow naturally.

I've seen a couple of the greats out there in clinics, and I've watched days and weeks of video of these natural horse folk at work, and I like to return and re-watch the best of these videos from time to time. Of course, picking up the ABCs of specific techniques is good, but more is involved. Repeatedly observing a guru work with horses allows you to gather a hint of something through osmosis—feel. The nonverbal stuff that happens while the guru works with a horse is what I mean. The slightest change in body posture or hand motion may only become evident the tenth, twentieth, or hundredth time you watch it.

Which brings up another good point—that these brilliant horse people doing the best work in the country didn't just wake up one morning as horsemanship gurus. Every one whose story I've ever heard put in years with horses and the teachers they could find to get where they are. Some certainly were born with natural aptitude for horsemanship, but each can tell of the painstaking labor he or she endured, the stalls mucked and wrecks survived, to get better with horses. It's comforting to think that they are human too and that any of us can improve if we apply ourselves. We all have the capacity to find feel.

So now when someone talks about "feeling of" a horse, I smile instead of wince. The words ring melodiously in my ears, rather than striking the discord they once did. Not because I'm on the inside of the group that can *feel of a horse* (no, that's out there somewhere still in the future), but rather because I've caught glimpses of it and can enjoy the journey with my horses. When there's a breakthrough, it's experienced together. When there's a setback, I'm getting better at fixing it, and my horses trust me more each time we work through problems. You'll not hear anyone other than natural horse folk say "feeling of," and that truly reflects that there's only one specific relationship on earth it speaks of—a special relationship between horse and human.

CHAPTER SIX

GROUNDWORK

GROUNDWORK—THE TERM SEEMS PRETTY self-explanatory in a general sense: working with a horse from the ground, right? True, but there are myriad variations of groundwork that produce as many results. In natural horsemanship, groundwork is ground zero; it's where the odyssey begins.

Before I'd been around natural horsemanship, I always assumed *riding* was what people did with horses, not messing around with them on the ground. Busting broncs like in the movies came to mind, not a series of nonviolent exercises done from the ground, allowing a person before long to ease into the saddle and move off on a horse that already understands some cues by the time he is mounted.

It seems my assumption wasn't too far off the reality of how many people get their colts going. Suffice it to say, the term "breaking" a horse is widely used in the mainstream, and for good reason. Many respected clinicians of the Better Way substitute terms like "gentling," "starting," and "beginning" horses for equally good reasons, and it all starts with *groundwork*.

Groundwork, as the term is used in natural horsemanship, doesn't describe whatever haphazard things a person might do with a horse from the ground, but rather a specific set of un-mounted exercises done with a horse to communicate with the equine and improve the relationship between horse and human in carefully planned stages. Likewise, groundwork sets up conditions with farther-reaching benefits than just to get a horse moving around with you on the ground, including trust, respect, and refinement of movements that translate directly to how a rider will work with the horse when in the saddle.

Groundwork is so important that even as a beginner witnessing in person and on video dozens of horse starts (and restarts), I wouldn't consider getting on a horse before being able to go through a range of groundwork exercises with passing grades. Clinician Pat Parelli calls it a "preflight check," and while I don't like the connotation of "preflight," there is more chance of "flight" being part of the deal if you don't do the "pre-check" part. Essentially all respected clinicians agree not only on the fact that groundwork is *the* key to safely training a horse, but that some combination of these exercises should be done every time before you ride. If it is your horse you are about to ride, groundwork tunes up the minds of both horse and rider and reestablishes the

Parelli Friendly Game, which consisted of just putting my hands on the horse and rubbing him pleasantly all over, took courage. Something had awoken within me even at this early stage, though. I became completely drawn to this horse. That link continually pulled me to the paddock, and I spent hours just hanging out with Niji—coffee in the morning sitting on the fence with him, coffee in the afternoon sitting by him on a stump—and eventually a relationship emerged that brought around my relaxation in his presence and being able to scratch him in various spots comfortably. Sure, at this point I thought I was training Niji to become used to human hands, but in retrospect it is easy to see that the bulk of the training that happened really was him showing me how to be around a horse. He was just fine all along.

What happens in groundwork is travel to another culture. You become an exchange student to the horse world. Groundwork exercises, whichever ones you end up doing, are a foreign language you try to learn—getting better at them with your horse is becoming proficient in the language of that land. At first it's pretty rocky. A beginner's movements are uncertain. If the horse is a beginner as well, he doesn't know what you are asking at first either. Spending plenty of days getting caught up in the spaghetti of a chaotic lead rope is just one of the joys of learning horse grammar. For me, getting my feet stepped on was as well, and looking back I now know that was *my* fault; I actually set myself up and then *asked* the horse to step on my foot, though I didn't realize it at the time.

For me, the single greatest key to getting better with horses at first wasn't an exercise, but rather an *understanding*. Groundwork wouldn't have been effective if I had not learned a concept about the way horse societies work. This understanding is the very root system that provides what good horsemanship needs to grow. Horses are prey animals, the ultimate flight machines. Their survival has depended entirely on their ability to sense danger at a distance and run like crazy to get away. Unlike other prey animals, they don't even have horns to help protect themselves if backed into a tight spot. It's all about panic and flee first, worry about what it was later. Humans, of course, are the ultimate predators dominating the planet. Understanding the differences was the key to getting started with groundwork.

Harry Whitney, a popular clinician, put it this way when I was talking to him about whether or not it is a good idea to hand- feed treats: "Horses live in a negative reinforcement society." To him it didn't mean negative in the sense of punishment, but rather that horses never add things to a situation (what he called a positive reinforcement) like a treat for doing something. If a horse wants to get another one to go through a gate, Harry said, he will make that clear by applying pressure, usually through some type of posture. If the second horse moves in the desired way from that pressure, the first horse then relaxes and removes that pressure. That release of pressure is the indication that things went right, and the situation is back to normal and everyone can relax. "The horse doesn't then go pick some grass and give it to the other horse," Harry keenly pointed out. The image cracked me up, and I've never forgotten it.

The key point for me early on was that horses have an entirely different understanding of the world than we do. I had to be told this; I really didn't know or think about it before. By observing how they act in a herd, humans can mimic some of those horse ways and get a better relationship with them, but the horses really never can understand much of how we humans do business amongst ourselves. Humans are capable of so many things that aren't part of a horse's makeup, like deception, backstabbing, and being on a schedule.

One significant difference between us and them is that they don't understand punishment in the same way. A horse relates actions to what is occurring at this moment. If you catch a horse at the instant he is acting out an undesirable behavior and apply a pressure of some kind at that moment, he may begin to associate the behavior with the pressure and choose to avoid it by stopping that behavior. However, if your horse does something you find unacceptable, and then five minutes later you get around to punishing him for it—like by lunging him for twenty minutes—the horse has no idea what is going on. He is back to assessing the world moment by moment for survival, taking in the environment. All punishment will do, especially if delayed from the event that spurred it by more than two seconds, is just make that horse begin to relate seemingly random unpleasant actions with you. The next time that horse sees you, don't be surprised if the bad behavior isn't worse and is combined with any number of other new not-so-great actions, like getting out of your vicinity quickly. In this instance, the horse has failed to relate the punishment to his own undesirable behavior and instead has related the punishment to you.

The way clinicians tend to speak about the language of horses is usually in terms of "pressure and release." This, the very skeletal structure of groundwork, is the vocabulary used to speak with horses. Parelli's games were a great way to get started. They were simple, fun, and really easy for a novice to grasp. Plus, Pat has a whole arsenal of stories, catchphrases, and jokes to help drive points home and get people to remember them. And, as is likely

the case with any beginning groundwork done properly, produced fast results.

It was incredibly rewarding when even the most simple requests got results at first. "It's all in the release," I had heard people say, and it was true. I began to get the feel for groundwork
with the most simple actions, and it was the release that made
them work and became the foundation that I built on. For example, if I wanted Niji to back up, I would put my fingertips on his
chest and press. The Parelli method discussed four phases of
firmness, where you begin lightly, then every few seconds up the
pressure until the horse figures out what it means. Then the release must come exactly as the horse figures it out. At first, as
Buck Brannaman says, you release for even "the slightest try."
The trick as a total novice was having enough awareness to recognize the slightest try. Then, hopefully, each time you repeat
the request, the horse should understand better and require less
pressure, and you should get better at asking as well.

Much of the understanding comes from hands-on experience. There's no way to get it without doing it. You can't do it as
a beginner without making some mistakes. There were times I
worried I'd ruined our horses by not getting a release right. Still I
forget to start light and initially ask my horses with too firm a request, which can create some resentment. Things go much more
smoothly when I make a conscious effort to ask in the lightest
way possible first. Some folks say the first request should be with
that ever elusive "feel"—that one should begin by trying to ask
without any outward cue, just an inward intention in your mind
of what you would like the horse to do. Of course, if you get a response that way, congratulations! Stick with it till the cows come
home. I haven't yet, though, and honestly pretty much forgot

about intention; it was hard enough for me just to remember not to start with a lot of pressure poking and pulling on the horse.

After I began getting the feel for a few groundwork exercises with Niji, Sokeri came along, and I had two horses to work with (or "play" with, as the Parellis would say). It was difficult to determine if I was boring the horses to death, if they liked these new interactions, or just what their state of mind was. I think it was more like, *Why are you interrupting my grazing/sleeping routine?* than *Oh boy, let's go play games*, coupled at first with, *Should I run from this poking, prodding weirdo?*

Slowly I began to improve from very modest beginnings. Getting both horses to back, move the front quarters, move the hindquarters, and lead better (using the same pressure and release methods when working in a halter) began to become as regular as feeding and hanging out. Spending time with the horse

Groundwork with Niji.

was a daily event, often many times a day. It was useful to be able to move the horses around in different ways when being around them, and I made a point to keep practicing these simple ground-work exercises even in informal settings.

Oddly, perhaps, some of the best help I received was from the horses acting up. You'd think that is the most undesirable situation to have with a horse, and I suppose it is, but every time I was forced beyond my quite conservative comfort zone, that zone increased in size. At first, for instance, I was really quite intimidated to get in the paddock with Niji and supremely careful to stay away from his massive business-end with its two hooves the size of howitzer rounds. Interestingly—in a purely scientific way—it wasn't long before he started to turn the hind end towards me to instigate a change in my position. I was easily manipulated this way, thinking it the right thing to get out of Dodge when he managed to get a bead on me, thus strengthening the undesirable and quite dangerous behavior.

At some point it dawned on me we had a problem here, although I don't remember thinking I was the cause, but rather that I needed to rectify this behavior in the horse. Summoning up extra courage, I began working towards changing our relationship with his hind end. Working ever closer to the hind end simply with pleasant strokes of the hand and curry comb came first. As long as Niji was not of the mind to put up a fight, he stood just fine for all this, and for me it was more just working over the fear of being around those back legs that helped. Carol showed me a trick using a rope to ask Niji to pick up his back feet, which worked great. I went from that to picking them up by hand, which was a whole new fear threshold. Then, I screwed up.

Niji and Sokeri were in a small paddock by the house during some of that first winter. She was obviously showing with foal, and they were getting different types of grain and minerals. I fed them at different ends to separate them. If I put hay down with the feed tubs, usually Niji, who finished his spot of grain first, would tear into the hay and give Soke plenty of time to finish her much larger portion of feed. At this time, I had grown very confident with Niji in general. Between Carol's work with him and my own, I was able to move him around quite fluidly and seemed to have worked past the hind end standoff.

One morning I put the feed and hay down like usual, then went a small distance away to tend to some other livestock. I looked up and noticed Niji had quickly eaten his grain, gone over to Sokeri, pushed her away from her own tub, and was scarfing down the Mare and Foal grain. I jumped over the fence and ran at him shouting, "Hey you, get out of that!" waving my arms all the way, supremely confident I was the boss these days and he'd move away. The feed tub was in a corner of the fence, so in retrospect, his one option was backwards, which also happened to be the direction I was charging from. I guess I expected him to back a little, turn, and go off, or else I just wasn't thinking, but move he did. Niji came at me backwards. I clearly remember seeing the two U-shaped back feet at eye level. Somehow the gelding chased me in reverse, kicking at me with both back feet, all the way across the paddock. Before I knew it, I was over the fence, heart racing, and he was back finishing Sokeri's breakfast. Luckily, none of those kicks had landed. I'm certain he was having a serious conversation with me, and if he had actually wanted to land one, he could have easily enough. This was one formative lesson in the language of horses for me. The result was he got what he wanted—I knew it, he knew it, and I was sure I'd completely screwed up Carol's horse to the point of no return. *How will I ever get this straight now?* I wondered.

The answer was in the groundwork. After that man-made incident, I figured it was do or die. Either I would assert myself in relationship to his hind end, or he would be able to manipulate me in many situations and, in his mind, not have to do as I asked sometimes. If I had avoided this incident, we probably could have forged ahead with regular groundwork activities and continued making good progress. But now, I had created a new problem that would be more difficult to overcome. I quickly put at the top of my list of things not to do with horses, *Never Create New Problems By Scaring, Cornering, And/Or Being An Idiot Around Your Horse.* I realized that if I had gone around the outside of the fence and asked Niji to move away from both me and the dish to the open area of the paddock where he could have complete freedom and his hay awaited him, it probably would have gone fine. Or, if I had just let him have the stupid grain, which he had pretty much finished by the time I got there anyway, I could have been more careful next feeding time and nothing would have come of it. Instead, in my mind I was the dominant one and went right at him to assert that position and had literally forced him into a corner. The joke was on me.

At this point, as you might guess, Niji was wary of me and kept the quick-turn-hind-end-kick option available at all times. Niji has always been a pretty willing and curious horse. Also, I had never hurt him, lost my temper around him, or been particularly inconsistent with him. I was just green and trying to figure things out, which was confusing to us both. He wasn't scared of me, just asserting himself as horses naturally do and finding the best way to be left alone (and get more grain).

The answer to my dilemma ended up being a little ground-work at liberty in the paddock. I had a coiled up rope with me, but did not put a halter on him, so he could leave at any time. Backing him was no problem. Neither was moving his forequarters. When I asked him to move his hindquarters away from me, this time by putting my fingers to his flank, I got the opposite response, and he pushed towards me and began to turn that back end my way. I smacked his rump with the rope and reinforced it with a "Yah!" This time there was plenty of open space, and he took off running away from me. I felt pretty bad about chasing him off. It seemed counterintuitive to chase him off when really what I sought was to have him calm and close, but this was the only way I could figure to change that lesson I taught him about how effective his rear end was regarding pushing me around. It wasn't long before he returned to check me out. I crowded his space and, as he went to turn his hindquarters to me, smacked his butt again with the rope and sent him across the paddock and down the hill.

This routine worked faster than I would have guessed. Later, after being exposed to round pen work, it became clear that what I had done with Niji was essentially the same concept. I decided when Niji could stand and when he moved his feet, also where his hind end could be. I kept him moving around the paddock until he would come and stand nicely without wanting to turn and threaten me with a kick. If he made a move to turn the hindquarters towards me, he consistently got popped with the rope in the butt and sent away. Truly, being in a tight space with him was pretty scary at first, but the experience of how to move him away with body language—and the realization that I actually controlled his feet when I did it right—helped me regain lost confidence. By taking care to do only as much as it required to move him out, I avoided creating any resentment. As Bill Scott would point out much later, by starting light with any request and then firming up, even the signals to move the hind end away, the choice is left up to the horse as to how much pressure you must escalate to get results. After a few pops with that rope on the rump, it only was necessary to motion towards the hind end to get him to move off; he knew the rope would make contact next if he didn't move it and get out of there. Working through this with Niji would be a major turning point in my ability to be comfortable handling horses.

Another major groundwork lesson came a little later. I spent a few months getting Sokeri to back, move fore- and hindquarters, come to me, lower her head, and pick up her feet. Some people can get this down in an hour, but I worked weeks and weeks on it before things seemed to be going pretty well. All these exercises were basically with the mare at a standstill, and I felt the need to move on to something more complex, like getting her to circle around me on the lead rope. I had seen the Parellis, Clinton Anderson, and some others do this with horses a thousand times on video, but I didn't seem to be able to quite get it to happen here in the real world.

I understood the basics. With the mare standing facing me, I would point with a hand holding the lead rope, look in that direction, then look back at her, and then start twirling the lead rope with the other hand. I twirled harder and harder, closer and closer and she just stood there. Then I would let the end of the rope start to pop her in the shoulder area. She wouldn't move, and it was uncomfortable for me to get any more aggressive. I tried this a bunch of times, but I probably made a fatal error when I backed down the first time and didn't get at least a slight try before quitting. Regardless, it seemed the amount of pressure was escalating to more than I should put on the horse, that I had to go beyond firming up to near aggression, and it just didn't seem right at the time. Afraid I might be on the wrong track somehow, I got Terrie to come over and work with me for a few hours.

"Show me how you work with her," Terrie said as we stood in our upper pasture, the coiled up lead rope and halter in my hand. "Sure thing," I replied and walked up to the bay and rubbed her down with the bunched up rope. Then I came around to her left shoulder, asked her to lower and bend her head slightly, and put the halter on, making sure to tie it correctly with the end that threads through the loop knotting back to itself rather than to the loop above—one of those simple things that is both helpful as it keeps the knot from overtightening and shows you've begun to acquire some horsemanship skills. Then I went about the exercises that I thought we had drilled to the point of perfection. Terrie watched from a distance as I bent Sokeri's neck each way, asked her to back from hand pressure on the chest, and asked her to disengage the front and rear to hand pressure. Then I asked her to back by shaking the lead rope. She backed (eventually), and I thought how great that maneuver was, as it was the closest thing to circling I could do.

"Hold on a minute," Terrie said. She came over. "Let me have that rope," she said. I stood back and watched. She began to shake the rope slightly, then *Wham!*, she snapped the lead rope hard. I was stunned. I'd never been that forceful. Soke raised her head and looked intently at Terrie like, *Where the heck did that come from?* Again, Terrie began to ask for reverse with a light shake.

Paying closer attention this time, I realized something that had been there all along, but that I hadn't seen in all the time I'd been working with the mare—she let her attention wander off. Instead of going right to backing, Soke moved her head to the side, her attention elsewhere, and *Wham!*, Terrie popped that horse's attention back again instantly. It only took three of those, and within a few minutes, Sokeri was paying full attention to Terrie, watching her with both eyes and both ears forward and firmly directed on her, and as soon as the lead rope began to move slightly, her feet began to move. That mare was ready to accept any request Terrie might give next and was on the lookout for it.

My requests, I realized, wondering how I couldn't see it before, had been more of a nagging, and thus the horse gave me a pretty wishy-washy response. Our conversation was more like, *Hey Soke, could you maybe back for me? Come on . . . I mean it . . . please . . . come on . . . nag, nag, nag . . . pretty please?* And she replied, *Who me? . . . Hey, look at that tree over there, it's moving a little . . . is that a dog I hear two miles away . . . nice day isn't it . . . hey, would you stop shaking that rope, it's attached to my halter, buddy.* If I got a step backwards, I thought that was great. To Terrie, a backwards step wasn't much, it was expected, and she could see straightaway that this mare was used to pretty much ignoring me in the hope that I'd just go away.

This lesson sticks with me for two big reasons. First, I realized what I hadn't realized—that my mare's attention was wandering when I tried to get groundwork exercises going with her. I did not see that her eyes, ears, and body posture were communicating something along the lines of, *Yeah, whatever buddy,* when I went to ask for her to move her feet. Terrie's lesson that day was the very beginning of an understanding of just how important every little gesture is to a horse all the time. Horses communicate with one another by the most miniscule motion of an ear, drop of the head, or slightest twitch of the tail. What I wasn't noticing was the equivalent of Sokeri holding a bullhorn to her mouth and yelling *WHATEVER!* right in my face.

The other lesson is that if we ask the horse to do something, from the beginning we must be willing to follow through with our request. That translates, if I decide it's time to begin working on backing my horse for the first time, I had sure better have allotted enough time to be there for my horse to accomplish the goal, and I need to be willing to work through any issues, including being quite firm at first, to at least gain a try from her.

In retrospect, what happened with Soke is a perfect example of how tremendously confusing it is for the beginner to grasp how one must be willing to escalate the firmness of a request to get a result, and yet at the same time, reward the slightest try. In a perfect world, I would have begun asking Soke to back just by thinking it, then a small wiggle to the rope, increasing the amount of wiggle until she took a step back from the pressure, at which point I'd release with perfect timing. Then, we'd repeat the process until I could ask with perfect lightness and get as many steps as I chose. What actually happened was twofold: one, I was too wimpy to follow through to get a try that I could see, which taught the mare to just hold out until I'd give up, and, two, I probably missed her initial slightest try, so she did not understand that going backwards was the answer to getting rid of the wiggling rope attached to her head.

When we goof up like this and a knowledgeable horsewoman like Terrie comes along to help us straighten it out, what we unknowingly have created is a situation that requires more firmness from the person to get things fixed than would be needed to get things started right in the first place. Since I unintentionally let Sokeri's attention wander toward whatever she liked rather than paying attention to me and my requests, when it was time to get down to business, I had reinforced the opposite reaction in her than was being sought. If I had been a better hand from the beginning, her dullness to requests never would have been established. I just didn't know. That's why Terrie had to be so forceful with her. On a good note, it only took a few of those serious attention getters to steer us in the right direction, and I realized firming up with my horse sometimes might be uncomfortable for me, but is really better for her. By being too nice, I had caused a problem that in the long run made it much harder on Sokeri to get straight. She was a bit spoiled.

A few days passed, and Sokeri and I went through the various exercises we always did each day, but the results were much different. She responded more lightly, and now I better understood that not only are certain body movements like backing and disengaging the hindquarters important, but I was watching for signs of respect and attention in her subtler body language, like eyes and ears, as well.

With this new-found understanding and the basics going quite well, I decided to go back to the circling attempt. I backed her a couple of steps, then, as she faced me, I began to ask her to circle, just as before. It was obvious she didn't understand, but she began to try and figure it out. When I popped her with the end of the lead rope and she took a step away from the pressure of it, I instantly stopped twirling the rope and stroked her neck, telling her how great that was. We regrouped, started over from scratch, and this time she gave me two steps. Then, it was like the flood gates of understanding opened up. The next time, starting again from scratch, I only had to twirl the rope, and she stepped off and began circling. She went all the way around me. I was so ecstatic, I nearly spontaneously combusted right there on the spot. Joy, excitement, and fulfillment welled inside me all at once. The triumph in that moment seemed equal to selling my first article or actually getting through college. It proved that I could get complex communication going with my horse, and that it was possible for this old dog to learn new tricks. It was absolutely exhilarating, and I rode that wave for two days until we ran slam into the next problem—but that's the way it works. Every advancement is a step in learning to get better with horses, with plenty of steps below that you've climbed up and many ahead still to climb.

These days, with more experience behind me, including some riding experience, I can't imagine not going through groundwork initially when working with a horse. So much about the horse can be revealed through groundwork—attitude, issues, and physical problems. The exercises are helpful in the sense of establishing cues and getting the horse to move certain ways, but the greatest benefit to groundwork is founding the mental relationship between horse and human and becoming more proficient as a human with pressure and release. If you can speak well with the horse on the ground in his own language, you are a hundred times more likely to communicate well with that horse in the saddle. But the real thrill for me is breaking through to the new level, like the circling, and it was groundwork that brought me to the understanding that those breakthroughs occur when the human advances in understanding. The key is adapting in ways that the horse can understand.

CHAPTER SEVEN

THE SLIGHTEST TRY

BUCK BRANNAMAN IS A VERY WELL-KNOWN clinician who likely has helped as many people and horses as just about anyone with his rigorous clinic schedule and renowned talent and sensibilities with horses. While I haven't yet met this famed horseman, he has helped me as well. I've read his books and seen a few of his videos, and while there are several points in my horsemanship where he has made a difference through these media, none is more apparent than my ability to mount Sokeri from the fence (or any other elevated spot, like a truck bed or stump). It is a perfect example of how a decent video can make a difference for the aspiring seeker of the Better Way.

This mounting from the fence video is a snippet tacked onto the end of one Brannaman did on round pen work. In fact, I came across it quite by accident when the video I was watching changed from the round pen setting to him standing by a fence with a mare saying, "I have yet to get bucked off a fence, but there's a first time for everything." He climbed up and sat on the fence with the lead rope in his hand, and I watched intently.

The mare was completely unfamiliar with the process of a rider mounting from the fence. In this short section of the video, Brannaman got her to understand that when he sat on the top rail and lifted the lead rope or rein straight up—maybe bumping it up as well—that she was to come alongside the fence, stand quietly, and allow him to slip into the saddle.

Mounting from a fence has the benefit of being physically easy on both horse and rider. We don't wrench the horse around as badly, and we don't stress our own bodies as much either. This is particularly helpful with horses and people already experiencing some physical issues. Additionally, it is always useful to have multiple options available for the various circumstances real life throws at us. But what I realized in those fifteen minutes or so of watching Brannaman work so that mare understood his request was much more profound for me.

Before I saw Brannaman get this mare in synch with him for mounting from the fence, every other bit of pressure and release I'd witnessed or worked on myself had been more direct and easily understood by the horse. For instance, if you hold the lead rope at the bottom of the halter, thumb down, and apply downward pressure, it won't be long before the horse drops her head seeking a release, and you're getting somewhere. Or, for instance, if you stand in front of the horse and ask her to back up and she doesn't, then you put pressure on by shaking the lead rope, which begs the horse to try backing up to move *away* from the pressure. Most of the basic maneuvers with horses are like this, where the applied pressure makes the desired outcome pretty obvious. But if you just sit on top of a fence and hold up on the lead rope . . . well, that's a pretty random request. The obvious thing to the horse, if it is like the other cues taught to that point, would be to go up. But there's a whole issue of gravity that makes it pretty hard for the horse to do that. So, she has to go searching through basically every movement at her disposal to figure this one out.

As part of the process, Brannaman did work on setting the horse up to win by trying to bring the horse around parallel to the fence first to begin a relationship to the lead rope being in the "up" position. At first, the mare ended up stepping perpendicular to the fence heading in the opposite direction. Then, as she began to try and sort this out, she moved her hindquarters, and Brannaman released the pressure on the lead rope: first for moving the hind end even a step, then for moving closer to the fence. Before long, as that mare got real close to the right position, he was releasing and stroking her neck in praise. But still, even with the master horseman making it look easy, it seemed like a tough bit of communication to work out.

It was pretty astounding to witness a mare with no clue about what was being asked of her when the halter rope was lifted to work out that this meant to bring the hindquarters around in position to be mounted. She had to sort through a range of possibilities to gain the right series of releases to put it all together. It was so complex, and yet on video it worked out in a short time. I truly felt from that point on there was really no limit to what the horse and human could communicate to one another if the human handles it right. I had to try mounting from the fence with Sokeri.

The first thing to enter my mind when I thought seriously about heading out to work on this with Sokeri was that once you start applying pressure to communicate with a horse, you're committed to the task. You have got to follow through on the new request until at least *the slightest try* is achieved. It is absolutely essential. If you tire out before the horse gets it figured out, you haven't just failed, you actually have taught the horse the very *opposite* of what you set out to do. The next time you try to get it straight will be even more difficult, because the horse will think, *But you released for this other thing last time, what do you want?* I wanted to work on this fence mounting lesson with Sokeri, but I worried about its complexity and how long it might take and my ability to pull it off. I didn't want to end up with a big fiasco on my hands. At the very least, I figured I should pack a lunch and have the afternoon clear if Sokeri and I were to get it straight.

Sokeri was already familiar with some basic pressure and release activities, which I knew would work in my favor. If Sokeri hadn't understood there was going to be a release from that halter being in such an obnoxious position, her tolerance might be zero, and the chances of her being willing to think her way through the situation equally small. The other fact in our favor was that I was so certain of the difficulty level of this, I was prepared to work at it as long as it took.

I haltered Sokeri, went through a bit of the basic groundwork we do to get the communication between us tuned up, led her over to the round pen, and climbed up on the fence. At this point, I had ridden her very little, but we had gone through a year of groundwork. I was really working to push through my own misgivings about riding her and horses in general. So I didn't saddle her; saddling might have helped to cue her into an intent to ride, but I wasn't thinking that way at the time.

Sokeri stood facing me, perpendicular to the fence. I tried to get her closer to the position I was looking for first, but as the mare from the video, her hind end swung away from the fence. With a deep breath I lifted the lead rope and tried to keep the image in my mind of what I was asking of her. She took it pretty well in stride at first, just standing there. After a bit I lifted a little harder, putting more pressure on the rope to try and "get through to her feet"—that is, until the horse moves her feet (or sometimes just a foot) in response to pressure. Sokeri just stood there, however. I began to worry that she might not get it. The image of me sitting there an hour later in the same fix had to be ousted from my mind. The blood totally left my arm, and I changed to the other one to keep the pressure consistent. Then the blood ran out of that one and I was out of arms, so I had to use them both to keep the rope up.

One interesting point I'd forgotten during my first attempt was that in the video Brannaman had bumped up on the lead to create more pressure. Some clinicians seem to like the bump as a useful way to ask for a response, while others say bumping is a series of releases that just confuse the horse—I don't know. In my experience, if I just can't seem to get through in one way, I try another. Typically, though, I don't use much bumping. This situation with Soke might not have taken as long if I'd remembered about bumping up, but who knows? I just held up on that rope, determined not to let her down (both figuratively and physically).

I began to feel sorry for her. In that position, the halter angle was pretty uncomfortable, and I had to overcome the desire to stop causing her discomfort before we broke through and at least initiated some kind of a try on her part. Finally, she began to fidget around; the lead was starting to get through to her feet, so I released and started over. Bill Scott later taught me one of the greatest perspectives in situations like this, which is that once the horse understands you are communicating through pressure and release and she recognizes what you are asking, it is the horse who decides how much pressure is required to begin moving in the desired direction. This places a heavy burden on the human to *always be consistent* in any request of a horse, to start softly with just feel and only then gradually up the pressure of the request as needed, being prepared to do as much as is needed but as little as it takes, so the horse truly has options and makes the decision.

Consistent handling during the asking/release is probably the most important aspect of the progress we humans can make in working with horses. I believe I am now at a rudimentary stage in my ability to apply pressure and give a perfectly timed release and hope there will come a time when I am able to reduce the initial pressure of my communication with horses. Sokeri likely would respond to softer pressure now if I were capable of figuring it all out. This has everything to do with *feel*, I'm sure. At that time, though, I felt like a real jerk holding my horse's head up and thought that she might just say, *Heck with you buddy, you're not my friend and I'm getting another human.*

Then she took a step. It was in the opposite direction than I was hoping for, so then I had a new dilemma on my hands . . . *Do I release for a step in the wrong direction to show that moving the feet is good, or does that teach her to go the wrong way? And is there really a wrong side to mount from or is that just some dumb human thing about cavalry guys and the side the right-handed men wore their swords on, so I shouldn't worry about it anyway? And what if my arms fall off from holding the lead rope in the air and I can never ride again?* By the time I sorted through these thoughts, the moment to release was lost anyway, so I held out. Luckily she came around the other way a step, and I instantly released and gave her some much appreciated loving and support. Then I lifted that lead rope again . . . starting softly. It wasn't long before she took another step around in the right direction and won a ready release.

This took awhile, and that day she got pretty good at getting up against the fence when asked with the lifted lead rope. I stroked her plenty for it and even rubbed her along her back on the side opposite the fence with the foot and leg I eventually would slide across her to mount. Then we quit work for the day. My confidence soared. Getting something like that going with Sokeri felt like a huge milestone. Winning some event couldn't have felt any better than the feeling of accomplishment I experienced from getting such an understanding going with this mare. It may seem like such a small thing to some folks, but not to me. I had communicated, in a positive way, the most complex request to my horse I'd ever attempted. She had understood me. We had gotten something going together that I was completely unsure I could manage. She had worked with me, and my ability to read her and release in the right way was put to a real test that day. The work it required was more challenging than many things I had yet done with her, and the fulfillment was equally great.

Enthusiastically, I spent the next several days building on that foundation. She began to move easily into position along the fence at the lightest lift of the lead rope. Now, I was faced with a personal threshold—all this was preparation to *get on her*, and now that she had done her part, it was time for me to do mine and get on.

Sokeri was totally mellow. She came to me a broke trail horse, although quite young at about three and a half years old. The angst about mounting had more to do with recently coming off of Niji, combined with some natural apprehension about getting onto a large animal, than anything to do specifically with her.

I pretended not to be scared (for what it was worth. I knew she would know anyway, but I hoped she would appreciate the effort), lifted that lead and got her in position, slid that leg across her back and rubbed her with the heel of my boot like I had been doing, and this time slid all the way over and onto her back. Then

Before mounting, I got her used to the feeling of my leg on the opposite side.

I started breathing. I rubbed her neck, got back onto the fence, and repeated the process. She just stood there, no problem, looking pretty uninterested, to tell the truth. I began to relax. The next time I slid onto her and sat for a moment, I rubbed her neck, and she decided to walk off.

Well, I wasn't prepared for this, but there I was, riding my horse, her in control and me somewhere between exhilarated and freaked out. For every great breakthrough there sure seems to be an equally great new challenge looming just beyond. I remembered the one-rein stop, and it was easy since holding the lead rope was pretty much like having only one rein. I pulled it and she bent her neck; her hindquarters swung around and she went from the frightening pokey walk to a complete stop.

I beamed for a week.

CHAPTER EIGHT

THE ROUND PEN

IT WASN'T LONG IN MY EXPERIENCE with horses before I became acquainted with the round pen. I began to notice both permanent wooden versions of this type of corral made from oak boards as well as temporary ones built from interconnected metal gate panels. These I saw in videos, in books, and even in real life as I drove around the area here in Virginia. I could tell they were at least very popular, if not downright essential to working with horses.

On several occasions early on in my quest to get better with horses, however, I heard Terrie say that round pens can "ruin a horse." This sentiment was echoed by other sources as well. It had a cumulative effect on me—it worried me. Then I realized it's not the round pen that ruins a horse, but how a person uses the round corral that can worsen a horse's condition rather than improve it—and one doesn't even need a round pen to do that. It was clear enough to me already that improperly timed releases could bring about the opposite result one sought when working with a horse. I could only imagine the consequences of undertaking some badly misguided advice to use a round pen to punish or otherwise dominate a horse in the typical predatory way. Activity like chasing a horse in the round corral could easily make for an increasingly frightened and claustrophobic prey animal. Of course, it seemed like the round pen was central to many amazing results. On the other hand, simply buying a round pen and getting in it with your horse isn't magic that will solve your problems either. That must come from just plain getting better with horses wherever you work with them.

When I began to hear quite a bit of talk about the potential dangers of using a round pen, we didn't even have one, so there wasn't much threat of me having a whole new way to screw up my horses. It was obvious, however, that the round pen seemed to be at the center of much natural horsemanship work. Nearly every clinician uses them, and they show up in video after video and clinic after clinic as a favorite type of space to work in with horses. So, I figured there must be something to this setup.

As I watched more videos, especially of people like Buck Brannaman and Dennis Reis, who really used that round definition of space as an asset to starting colts and getting improvements with troubled horses, I began to see what an amazing help it can be to a capable hand. It seems that one great advantage of the cornerless round corral is how it allows the human to apply incredibly subtle pressure and release while a horse is free to move around continually. The round pen allows that flight instinct, which can be so overwhelming in a horse, an outlet. As the horse runs circles along the fence, the person can remain close enough to the horse to still conduct a body language and feel conversation with him. The horse can move and pay attention to the human at the same time, without running off. Actually, it might be more accurate to say the horse can run *until* he can pay attention to the human, who can stand there close by in the center of the circle and wait for the right moment to act.

Which is the crux of the matter. Knowing what to do and just exactly when to do it is essential. It's not too hard to see where a person might do more damage than good in the round pen if he is inexperienced and doesn't use the right vocabulary for that conversation with the horse. Getting a horse in a round pen and just running circles without knowing when to stop isn't going to improve your relationship with a horse. Add other tools, like a flag or coil of rope, to the situation, and the person who doesn't understand how to dial pressure on and off can traumatize the horse and end up with problems that can be pretty difficult to overcome. Even if a person might manage to get a horse "hooked on," where it wants to be with and listen to the human . . . then what? Buck Brannaman says of this situation in the round pen, "If all you can get out of this style of working with young horses is getting them to turn and look at you, it's just a party trick and you blend in with about a thousand other 'horse whisperers' around the world."

I'm not convinced a person can ruin a horse any faster in a round pen than on the end of a lead rope. It seems that first and foremost, running a horse in endless circles no matter where it is done is counterproductive. Longeing on a line or running circles in the round pen without support, purpose, and that ever important "feel" can make a horse dull, bored, and even resentful. At first a horse may even try to turn and hook on, but the misguided hand may say, "No, keep going! Run circles!" and before long the horse learns that the human wants to be tuned out and that the correct response is to only run in circles without thought. But if you present a sense of timing and meaningful purpose to the horse—which has to be learned firsthand from a teacher who has mastered it, coupled with direct experience—allowing the horse to run circles at first can be used to transform your relationship to your horse for the better.

One common misuse of the round pen is thinking of it as an exercise wheel laid horizontal. First, running a horse in circles forever as exercise may help with fitness in a physical way—although even here I've heard the argument that it develops only certain muscles and not others, thus misshaping a horse for real world situations, where work isn't always tightly circular—but still creates the mind-numbing situation described above. We have to consider that the brain is never separated from the body of the horse, just as with humans. The horse is intelligent, needs mental stimulation, and is guaranteed to tune you out—if not begin to develop a negative attitude towards you—if you offer him only circles to run each day.

Many of us surely remember sitting in some concrete block, windowless, fluorescent-lit classroom with an incredibly dull teacher trying to learn some subject that just became torturous after a short while. I'm sure it's just like that for the horse. One should always want the horse to pay attention to the human. That task is made infinitely easier if you provide interesting exercises for the horse, changing things up so he needs to watch you and see what comes next. It's a lot more fun for the person as well. That's why Parelli calls his groundwork "play" and those exercises "games"; it's an active effort on his part to convey just how central avoiding boredom is to good horsemanship. Harry Whitney has mentioned the same thing to me. He's convinced that the average person suffers chronic loss of imagination beginning somewhere in the late teens and that reinvigorating creativity when working with horses is a key to much success.

The second problem has to do with trying to tire a horse as a training method. Sometimes, people attempt to fatigue a spirited horse with the hope of then being better able to work with him. The problem with this theory is that horses increase their fitness rapidly. You might tire a horse by running him in the round pen for ten minutes today, but in a few days, you won't wear him down in ten; it'll take more. Before you know it, you'll be spending half the day trying to tire the horse. It's much better to just start working on the relationship from the get-go. If you have a strong, positive relationship with your horse, whether he's spirited or not, that horse will tune in and listen to you as a respected leader.

One day Carol happened by a horse-stuff liquidation sale at a house on a back road not far from our farm. When she saw a round pen with a three-hundred-dollar price tag, she came and found me, and we immediately made arrangements to buy it. The pen consisted of thirteen red metal pipe fence panels that interlocked with three gates to make about a 50-foot-diameter circle. A few days later we rode over in the farm truck, loaded it up, and returned home, where we set it up in the upper pasture as it came off the truck.

Right away I noticed how useful it was. I put Niji in it at feeding time so he wouldn't steal Sokeri's grain if I wandered off to do something besides stand guard. My horse arrangement options had increased!

As for actually *using* the new addition to our training toolbox, at first it was Carol who got the most use out of it. Once in the round pen, she almost immediately took the halter off Niji, and the two of them worked "at liberty," with results that just astounded me. The very first day, she had him following her movements. When she walked, he walked. When she'd circle in the middle of the pen and hop along in a trot-like skip, Niji responded by trotting around the outer edge of the round pen. I was in awe, and totally entertained. Whereas I was more fearful of making mistakes and took baby steps with Sokeri, Carol was just having fun with her horse, with great results.

After about a week of this round-pen-at-liberty play, she laid a couple of plastic 55-gallon drums on their sides end to end against one panel of the pen, like a minute hand on a clock. The Parellis do this quite a bit. Pretty soon the gelding followed her around, completely at liberty, and jumped those barrels. They had great fun and made wonderful progress; the round pen had liberated them by eliminating the connection of rope and halter. Carol used no equipment at all, no sticks or ropes, and I'm sure that it was "feel" she got going with Niji to achieve those results. This round pen allowed a space where they could move together, yet it was well enough defined that Niji couldn't just decide *Heck with this* and leave. It worked for them.

For the longest time, for me, the round pen was just a good place to go and work with Sokeri on the halter and lead. It was the perfect means to escape from the still-nursing, and often cantankerous little Whipper Snapper and yet still allow them to remain close enough to avoid anxieties that could have been quite counterproductive. Entering the round corral also seemed to indicate to Soke to shift gears. When inside, it was time to focus on building our relationship through groundwork. A little later, it was really helpful for my early experiences in the saddle. Since the space was small and well defined, I had more confidence to concentrate on various maneuvers, since it was a given that she couldn't run off with me. Even if she wouldn't have, just knowing that she *couldn't* was reassuring.

As I got better with natural horsemanship, particularly after learning hands-on with a few capable horse folk, the round pen became a much more helpful tool for me. Particularly, clinician Bill Scott helped me to understand how to send a horse around, look for changes like an ear coming towards me and the head lowering, then turn my body to release pressure and allow the horse to stop, turn, and face me. It sounds easy enough, but knowing how hard to push a horse and then timing the release right is tricky. Getting better at this has been helpful with gaining the focus and respect of Niji and Sokeri, and even Whipper, who is just starting out with more advanced groundwork. I've even put Niji and Soke in together and worked with them at the same time, which is fun and challenging—focusing on sending one around, while keeping the other standing, for instance, really puts your ability to communicate specifics to a horse to the test.

The round pen also can be an aid for transitions with the horse. I found, for example, that if I got Sokeri or Niji walking around the round pen, then intensified and projected my energy and got them to move up to a trot, I was learning about feel. Also, projecting that energy toward different parts of the horse's body causes the horse to move in different ways. For instance, if you focus your energy on the horse's hindquarters, thinking it will push him to go faster, you may be surprised when he untracks them, turns, and faces you. Directing the forward pressure a little further up the horse, behind the front shoulder, creates a forward boost. These kinds of experiences were really beneficial and helped me to further understand how horses work. Making those up and down gait transitions smooth on the ground in the round pen translates to good transitions in the saddle. Of course, the positioning of horse and human are quite different, but the intention and relationship are the same, and that is what the round pen helps to develop, when used correctly.

Yet, I find I am using the round pen less as the horses and I progress and time goes on. I think the benefits are clear when we can allow horses the freedom to move and yet build communication with them. Not only is it a good place to start colts that are inexperienced with people, or work with those that have serious issues, it can be good for just tuning up a horse once in awhile. Now, Soke and Niji both tune in and listen to me or Carol wherever they are, which is rarely in the round pen these days, with or without a halter. Usually, sending them around once or twice each way is all it takes to get them "hooked on" and clearly focused on me. I use the pen occasionally as a tune-up, but it isn't a necessity.

Ultimately, having a horse become capable of real world activity is the goal. On my farm, I go riding for enjoyment, to check on fences, to pull logs, or to go feed and check on other horses. Riding in the round pen is fantastic when getting to know a horse. But, as things progress, my need and my desire to spend time in the little round corral diminishes because there's a whole world outside of it to ride in.

CHAPTER NINE

GOING BAREFOOT

TERRIE WOOD AND I DISCUSSED AT LENGTH many points about natural horsemanship, from the round pen right on down to the most basic maneuver like picking up a horse's feet. Even though she was the key to our getting started in the Better Way with horses, exhibiting amazing patience in person and on the phone, enduring hours of discussion, months would pass before the term "barefoot trim" or the realization that Terrie was an able barefoot trimmer would come to my attention. Carol knew about this information well before me, and it was her occasional mention of it that began to sink in and take hold in my consciousness. At some point the understanding struck that she was talking about the horses not just going unshod, as they had been for some time, but getting a barefoot trim (a special type of trim that was as much a part of Terrie's overall work as boarding horses and teaching natural horsemanship).

Ever since our horses came home to the farm, Carol and I both used a good friend as our farrier, who handled them well. Both horses arrived with shoes, which we immediately had removed as we intended to stick to groundwork on easy pasture footing for some time. Even lacking technical understanding of the "barefoot trim," we knew our horses did not need shoes to hang out in the fields, or even to go riding in the environment here.

Neither Niji nor Sokeri had any problems with the regular trim they received from our farrier. After about a year, though, Niji began to toe-in on one of his front legs. It was very slight and may have had nothing to do with the trim he received, but was another consideration for Carol, who increasingly spoke of getting Terrie over to try this "barefoot trim." Now that I was aware of the term's more specialized meaning, I also realized that much talk and controversy seemed to surround it. Curiosity built in me to see how it would do on our horses—was it really all that different? Then opportunity arose: the horses were due for a trim, and the regular farrier didn't make it out as scheduled. We had Terrie come over to trim both horses.

Terrie's approach had a different feel, but knowing how Terrie is with horses, that was no surprise. She seemed to connect with the horses—not just to look at the hoof in front of her, but somehow to bend her tactics to the needs of the whole horse. While I never was displeased with how the other farrier handled the horses, the process was more of a job with him. Each foot was taken in the order he chose, regardless of how the horse felt about it. This may be a small thing, but Terrie took care, with Niji in particular, who was more finicky about holding up his feet, to start with a leg he felt the most secure having worked on, then building confidence with the others as she made her way around. This and similar considerations required extra time on her part—her concern wasn't simply to get a decent trim done and then be on her way to her next trim, but to make certain the whole horse was well, to work towards increasing the horse's relationship towards the human (particularly where picking up the feet is concerned), and even to take time with us to better our technique of using pressure and release to get some finesse into our horses' leg lifting.

Terrie says a large percentage of her business comes from horse owners who either no longer can stand the battle they have with a heavy-handed farrier or whose horses are troubled and the regular farriers have given up on them. It's poignant to consider Terrie, a thin, small-framed woman with an easy demeanor, coming in to trim horses that big, burly, experienced male farriers won't touch. It's proof that the relationship with the horse is paramount and that the horses aren't inherently "troubled." Rather, it is understanding and communication on the human's end that's missing in the relationship, and the trouble is human-made.

Terrie shared with us a predicament she found herself in that explains this perfectly. She drove a couple of hours to trim several horses new to her, and a barn manager was supposed to be on site to assist. She found the stable, but no help, and couldn't raise the owner on the phone. Rather than quit and drive all the way back, she decided to go ahead and trim. The first stall housed a mare, and she was not about to be haltered, let alone have her hooves trimmed, so Terrie retreated. Another mare, and a similar situation awaited in the next stall. She was about to call it quits, but went for the third stall—a gelding who behaved perfectly for her. Encouraged, Terrie trimmed her way through the other horses without much trouble and finally arrived back to the first two mares.

"They were so sensitive," she explained. "But I listened to those horses until they gave me permission to work on them. If you listen to the horse and adjust with her, eventually she will work with you the best she can." Terrie believes many of the problems farriers have come from them not listening to the horse or having the patience required to establish the relationship necessary for a good, safe trimming experience. She says that often after an initial visit working through a trim with a horse who is challenging, follow-up visits rarely present any problems for her.

Aside from Terrie's good feel working with our horses, the barefoot trim itself kindled my curiosity. Our horses had been trimmed several times without shoes since arriving. How could simple trims vary enough to have their own titles? Terrie had the horse lift a foot, she held it against her thigh on the thick farrier's chaps, then removed one tool or another from the various pockets and pointed out to us what was going on with the horse in that foot and how the new trim would work.

The idea for the natural trim derives from studies of horses in the wild. To make matters even more complicated, different styles of barefoot trim exist, and the apples/oranges factor abounds in this realm. It can be really difficult to get a clear understanding of just what you are getting when you ask for a barefoot trim if you don't have a Terrie Wood in your neck of the woods to explain it. Sometimes the trim also is referred to as a "wild horse trim" or a "mustang trim." The latter term is also used to refer to a slightly

Terrie and two of her barefoot horses.

different trim, which only snubs off the toe of the hoof without creating the other aspects of the trim Terrie gives.

Generally speaking, for the barefoot trim, the farrier essentially mimics on a domestic horse's hooves the wear it would experience if it were running in the wild on a hard surface, the theory being that Nature works out what's best for the animal. Some studies found that the heels need to be kept short while the rest of the hoof growth is trimmed back proportionally, and Terrie nipped and rasped great examples for us. The finished foot looked oddly petite to me at first. The regular mainstream trim typically leaves the horse standing higher on the heel while shortening the forward hoof growth. A hoof with the barefoot trim, the theory goes, provides a more natural and therefore healthy angle of foot placement. This translates into less stress on bones and tendons. I found after a few months that Terrie's trim maintained better. There definitely was less cupped area in the sole for stuff to get stuck in, which added to the curious fact that their hooves even seemed to remain harder than before, which was a miracle in the deplorably wet conditions spring brought that year to these Blue Ridge Mountains of Virginia.

After a trim, any horse is likely to be tenderfooted. It seems that after toughening up, though, keeping shoes off works out well for our guys. There's been no trouble keeping and riding the horses on the semi-rocky pasture here. Sokeri in particular seems a bit ouchy on the gravel roads on our farm, always wanting to walk off to the side (or in the ditch, or up the bank . . .). I hear many people never worry again about shoeing their horses after going barefoot, but if she were to be on gravel surfaces much each week, I probably would go ahead and try shoes on her to see if they made her more comfortable. Certainly staying away from shoes is less time consuming, avoids piercing the hooves with nails, is less costly, and reduces some potential problems during riding, like throwing a shoe. Hoof boot technology has advanced too, making them an option for those faced with riding a barefoot horse on particularly unpleasant surfaces, like jagged gravel, for short durations.

Terrie's trim is working great for us. The records show she's needed to come about every three months like clockwork. Several trims ago, she left a rasp for me, with a lesson on how to touch up the hooves in between trimmings. I've given it a try, but it's harder than she makes it look (I bet that rasp is just too dull!). Interestingly, the last two times Terrie has come out to trim, Soke has not needed it. This means her barefoot trim has now maintained a full six months, and it appears touching up may be all she needs from this point onwards. The art of full-fledged trimming is one I fully intend to avoid; it's one job I'm happy to pay to have done. Still, it's important to me to broaden my skills with my horses and be able to do all the basic things like a quick trim, give a shot, or deworm. Taking responsibility for my equine companions is part of that relationship I'm building. They know when you really put forth the effort to care for them.

From experience, I'm a believer that a decent barefoot trim in the Terrie Wood style is the way to go, and I pass that information around. Terrie admits, though, that her trims vary from horse to horse. "I've read and studied from the extreme to the less extreme," she says of the various hoof trimming practitioners promoting their particular beliefs on the subject. "It's still all just theory. I don't try to change angles to animate the gait," she explains, "I just try to balance the foot so the horse doesn't have to wear a shoe."

Many people, however, get so zealous about barefoot trimming they wage full-on war against shoeing, and even other types of trims. You won't have to click much online to see this firsthand, if you're curious. I've seen plenty of happy, healthy horses with shoes, and, like I said, I'll definitely try them on Sokeri if we end up riding much on gravel in the future. Likewise, I've seen perfectly content horses with a trim from a mainstream farrier as well. Most important is to make certain horses get foot care *period* ... sounds obvious, but so many horses get back-burnered in people's lives, and hoof care, it seems, is one of the first things that falls away. Having said all that, I believe feet trimmed to a shape they would wear to in the wild on a hard surface really does produce a more natural angle for the hoof, thereby improving the horse's overall structural connections throughout the legs and body. It is one thing I can do to provide the best care for my horses, in the spirit of keeping things more natural for them in this unnatural world.

CHAPTER TEN

DON'T GET ON!

AS PRETTY MUCH A BEGINNER in the world of horses and a fervent follower of the Better Way to the best of my ability, I relish the few instances where I come across absolutes. If, like me, you've devoured every scrap of information from the great horse folk out there you can get your hands on, you also know just how unusual certainties can be. Honestly, discovering any answer not prefaced with "Well . . . that depends," is about as likely as finding a Wade tree saddle in a box of cornflakes. But, I found one (not a saddle, but an absolute, and I should say my mare Sokeri pointed this one out to me). It is stated plainly in one of those horsemanship Bibles, *True Horsemanship Through Feel* by Bill

Dorrance and Leslie Desmond: "If your horse moves when you try to get mounted, don't get on!"

In a realm of horsemanship full of gray area, it doesn't get any more black and white than that. I savored that moment, for once knowing exactly what not to do in a situation with my horse, for about thirty seconds. Then the realization hit, THUNK! Of course, once discovering the horse likes to move when I think about mounting, so therefore I *won't* get on, what next? I'm left standing on the ground at this point, wondering where to apply pressure and release this time.

Sokeri came to me with the problem already entrenched in her behavior. I suppose, knowing her from more than two solid years of daily life together now, that she has a different idea about what's fun than a human does and it is her way of letting me know just that. She most likely spent time before coming here voicing that opinion in that way to other riders on the trail by practicing disengaging her hindquarters as soon as that first foot hit the stirrup. That bay, turning wicked circles with a young person hopping along hoping to get pulled up in the saddle and under way, is easy to visualize.

When I sought to get her to stand still for mounting up, all the respected voices agreed that to just jump ahead and get on anyway is *out of the question*! Jumping into the saddle at that point not only could get me hurt, but also would represent jumping over about ten issues dealing largely with respect. It sets up a bad precedent that could result in some far-reaching and potentially dangerous consequences if left unresolved. The fix suggested in the book and by Terrie was to keep the reins handy, stand at the horse's shoulder facing towards the back end of the horse, turn the stirrup, and get the proper foot in it.

Then, grab a handful of mane, give the horse an "Okay, I'm getting on now" look, and then step up and lean over the saddle belly down. The idea is to get into the saddle in stages, and at each one communicate to the horse you are getting on, so you are basically asking permission, or at least being considerate of the horse. If the horse communicates it isn't ready or doesn't give permission, then hopping back down, regrouping, and giving it another go is the general rule. You might also double check your tack to make certain nothing is out of place, poking or pinching the horse.

It might seem that not getting on because *the horse* doesn't give permission is allowing disrespect to go unchecked. Or that getting back down in response to an undesired behavior reinforces it. The point, though, is that we are trying to create a willing partner in our horse. If we force an issue like mounting the horse when she isn't ready, then we resort to dominating her. That isn't a foundation for lightness and good communication, but can cause bracing and resentment. Besides, it may not be disrespect anyway. It may be misunderstanding at first. The repetition in asking the same way each time, several times, takes us to a point where we know the request no longer is misunderstood. If, as in Sokeri's case, it persists on and on, then it may be the horse saying she'd rather not have you aboard. So the advice for me was to try to step up into the stirrup, and when she moved to take a step, hop back down, gather up the reins, and back her up a few steps. Then repeat. Eventually the backward steps should communicate holding still for the stepping up. In this situation, because of the consistency, all that tiresome backing may prove a bigger hassle to the horse than just standing still for you to get on—therefore making the right thing easy.

The sack-of-potatoes position.

Once the horse stands still for the sack-of-potatoes position, where you are in one stirrup and leaning across the saddle, stroke her neck and say nice things. Voila, the problem should be worked out. Of course, I couldn't even get this far with Sokeri. I hopped down and backed her a hundred thousand times, and the mare wasn't giving any permission, period. So the advice for me was to try to step up into the stirrup, and when she moved to take a step, hop back down, gather up the reins and back her up a few steps. Then repeat. Eventually the backward steps should communicate holding still for the stepping up.

I did this.

And did this.

And did this, and did this, and did this, and got frustrated, went and did something else, came back and did this. And then did this some more . . . .

I'm not kidding. It took so long I figured I must be doing something wrong (even though it would be pretty doggone hard to mess up backing a horse a few steps with the reins). *Perhaps the mental challenge is too much for me*, I began to wonder. I guess I expected the few steps back to be some silver bullet answer to the problem, like one of those TV clinics where in thirty seconds a fidgety horse running all over its owner is suddenly transformed into a charming, willing buddy with the change from a web to a rope halter. Nope, not in my life. But, slowly, very slowly (so slowly that to this day Sokeri has probably taken more steps backwards in the reins than forwards), she began to stand still when I would step up onto that first leg of the trip into the saddle. I think she may have liked the neck stroking in particular, which came regularly when she gave a hint she might be thinking about maybe standing still (called "rewarding the slightest try," often the first step to a horse sorting out a handler's new request) but not when she moved that foot. Finally, she stayed still when I stepped up. Then throwing my other leg over and getting it into the stirrup wasn't a big deal.

After the breakthrough and for nearly a year afterwards, she would stand really well for the mount and for about twenty seconds after. Once I would get situated, though, she still had a tendency to walk off without my asking for it. I always met this with stopping and then taking several steps backward. We started every ride pretty much going backward—I'm sure we both began to think it might actually be forward after awhile. My thinking was, if reverse worked when she moved off while I was mounting, it should work for stepping off after just mounting—but it didn't. I mean it really didn't; not for six months of trying, and I was extremely vigilant with the consistency. I did, however, get it figured

Finally, Sokeri stood still while I mounted.

out some time later, and it was Bill Scott, a clinician from Otto, North Carolina, who gave me the key. Of course it took a month for me to realize I had the key the whole time. And once I figured it out, it only took fifteen minutes to fix the problem, but that's another chapter.

The lesson for me from Sokeri's mounting ordeal was not just getting past the moving off, but having another set of expectations shot to pieces. Perhaps it is just a human contrivance to expect certain outcomes, like getting beyond a snag with your horse in less than a month of steady work. The few horses I've been blessed to know so far have shown me they are ready to get beyond snags when I get it right and put the time in, however much that may or may not require. Really, it is the horse that has the patience, waiting and waiting for the human to get the obvious accomplished so they can get on with things. The mettle required of a horse to teach a human must be astounding.

Which leads to another difficult experience I had in getting onto a horse, this time with Niji. Unlike Sokeri, Niji was green under saddle. When he first came to our place, he was incredibly willing. We kept him in a small paddock near the house with good shelter and switched him to a better pasture on nice days. After walking him half a mile to that upper pasture a few times, I got bold and hopped up on him bareback with only the halter and rope. This went extremely well for someone who had never even heard the term "groundwork" at that point and had zero hours on a horse for at least fifteen years. I must have done this a dozen times or so. Then, one day after a rain, and with my confidence building, I decided it was time to take a new route for a change of pace. There's an old farm road here that snakes around out of the way, but gets to the same place, so I figured it would be a short, easy trail ride.

Everything was going super, and he was certainly curious about the new route. We made our way along the two rocky wheel ruts of a road, down and around a nasty hairpin curve, and into a loamy valley. Here, the weeds had grown wild and were at least six feet tall. I thought, *Great . . . I'm up here and Niji can walk through them and I'll stay dry.* About the time I thought that, and we entered maybe ten inches into the weedy zone, the sensation of these stemmy plants rubbing along his sides began to scare him. He took off straight ahead. I was determined to stay on and took hold of his mane, which worked for about a second before I tumbled off the back of the horse into a heap on the ground.

He ran a couple hundred feet, then stopped to graze. I collected myself, stood up, and walked up to him. Now, even I had heard to always get back on the horse, so I did. Which went fine. I sat up there, and he seemed calm enough. Then I asked him to go. And he went. He went straight to bucking this time, and I was bucked off so hard I landed up a steep hillside where the road was cut into the mountain. My abused body ended up ten feet higher than the horse when it made contact with the ground. Niji ran, tail flagged, gorgeous gait, all the way home.

When I finally hobbled to the house, Carol stood there holding Niji by the lead rope. "Where you been?" I can still hear her. "I wondered what happened when Niji got here before you."

The lesson for that day is threefold: don't believe everything you hear, don't get on a horse before you and/or the horse are ready for it (note that you may not necessarily be the best judge of that), and try to be thinking ahead about things that might freak out your horse (like those tall weeds). I would get two of those three straight by the next wreck.

Not long after that, my education progressed far enough to learn about groundwork, and I realized that I had gotten ahead of myself. Carol worked quite a bit with Niji in the round pen, and I did hours of groundwork with him as well. Many months later, after I had begun to ride Sokeri with good success, I got bold again and decided to try saddling up Niji. He was at the house paddock, and I wanted to get him to the upper field where Soke and Whipper Snapper had been for a few days. He saddled up with no problem; he stood like a champ. In the gravel driveway, I went through the basic groundwork, bending his head each way, backing him, circling him . . . no problem. So I got in the saddle. I have to say, stepping up onto a horse that just stood still was so unusual after the challenges of getting on my mare that I relaxed and enjoyed the moment. Then he responded beautifully. He easily gave me lateral flexion to each side, moved the hindquarters when I asked lightly with my leg, and even moved the front quarters from a slight bit of leg pressure on the first try. He walked around the turning circle in our driveway with me aboard for ten minutes. This horse calmly, with head low and in a perfectly relaxed state, did everything I asked without fail. What a perfect time it would have been to stop and end on an absolutely fantastic note. But I didn't.

Carol came out to see how we were doing. "He's doing so well, I'll ride him on up," I said. "Why don't you come get me in the car." Niji and I headed down the road. He maintained the pokey pace I desired, being the novice rider I was.

Then, Carol started the car.

The noise of the car starting way back at the house triggered the flight response in Niji. It was so fast it is difficult to describe. One moment I was completely relaxed on a serene mount ambling along a beautiful gravel drive with trees towering overhead and birds singing just for us, the next nanosecond a thunderbolt catapulted out from under me and I was lying on my back looking up at the towering trees, seeing the birds laughing at what just happened. I heard ca-clop, ca-clop, ca-clop fade into the distance, and then the car stopped before running over me.

Niji hadn't tried to get rid of me. He was frightened, and the result of his panic was to run, and I wasn't capable of hanging in there with him long enough to provide the emotional support necessary to get him stopped and calmed. In retrospect, spending those really good first riding moments in a safe environment like a round pen almost certainly would have avoided the wreck; I blame myself and seek to provide that safe environment first now. I just didn't have the experience to realize how important it is and that I was compromising his progress by allowing such a large opening for problems.

Carol drove us to the upper pasture where Niji waited calmly, grazing outside the fence by the other two horses. I walked right up to him, got the lead rope, and took him through the pasture to the round pen. There the groundwork all checked out fine, and I mounted him again. He stood fine, and we did a few small moves, and then he bolted again and I flew off him, landing on my feet this time.

I knew enough about pressure and release at this point to realize I was teaching him that to get relief from the rider, just bolt! I also knew I wasn't capable of overcoming this problem at my level of experience. So it was back to groundwork, and there we stayed. I felt kind of bad about it. It seemed I was holding Niji back and a more capable horse person could get through this. But he had a great home otherwise, and I would see this through, however long it took.

Good preparation through groundwork is the way to build a solid foundation with the horse so that it will be comfortable with you as the rider. The better you can get with groundwork and riding in a safe and regular setting, the better you will be suited to handle the unexpected in an unusual setting. On the other hand, you can't just stay stuck in endless groundwork forever—there must be forward motion. All that circling and backing and leading and moving the horse's various parts is just the foundation for something else. Bill Scott, a clinician who would soon enter our world, has a great way to explain this. Say you went to second grade and had some trouble, so you were held back and made to take it again. The next year you got it pretty well and had a good time, but you were made to take it a third time. It was really no trouble at this point, as all the second grade work was review and easy for you now. So then you are held back again and again and again, say eight more times. Now, how do you think a horse feels if it is on its tenth year of second grade?

Being stuck there is monotonous, and it's not really fair to the horse. People must break out of their comfort zone to advance and grow, and I am no exception. After Niji was responding well to all the regular stuff on the ground (and I was no longer getting rope twisted around my various body parts by accident), it was time to move on to new horizons. The groundwork is preparation for riding, and horse and human both can become dull if no new challenges are attempted in a long time. So, when horse and human are ready, we must *get on*! Just remember that if your horse wants to move out when you try, *don't get on*! See? Simple.

CHAPTER ELEVEN

ANATOMY OF A WRECK

THE PHOTO THAT ACCOMPANIES this chapter is a snapshot in time representing a small moment of triumph in my work with horses. That moment from the first clinic I attended, as it would turn out, would be sandwiched between a whole bunch of effort to get Niji to accept me in the saddle beforehand and the fantastic wreck that followed shortly thereafter, making me locally famous for awhile and sending me again back to square one. But there, in that moment in black and white, I sit comfortably on Niji, supremely pleased with the results of much toil, experiencing a fulfillment that only comes from diligent persistence and making a real breakthrough in understanding with a horse. I rub his neck in praise of his acceptance of me swinging my leg over and sitting on him. Not only am I on top of the horse, I'm on top of the world!

Often after a disaster, a retrospective view provides a clear indication of the cause. This picture, I now see, shows exactly the cause that would send me flying a few minutes later, though it is impossible to see it without knowing the rest of the story leading up to the event.

Getting involved with this clinic happened quite suddenly. I saw an article in *Eclectic Horseman* about a clinician named Bill Scott. The piece caught my eye because he was riding a horse without any headgear at all—I wasn't interested in doing that bridleless riding myself—I was lucky to be able to ride *with* reins—but it was a curiosity. A sidebar explained he lived one state away in North Carolina. Most clinicians are out west, so the possibility of a capable teacher of the Better Way within driving distance really interested me. Carol hadn't heard of him before, but when I called to see if Terrie had, I got quite a surprise: Terrie hadn't met Bill before, but she had just lined him up for a weekend clinic at her place a few months off and was looking for riders.

How incredible! I thought of the coincidence. She needed riders who could canter and, now officially cantering with Sokeri, I signed up right then. I figured there ought to be an article or two I could get from the clinic as well, so I got Bill's number from Terrie and rang him up to see if he was open to the idea.

Within a day Bill and I spoke. Deriving an article or two from the upcoming clinic suited him fine, and I lined it up tentatively with Emily Kitching, the editor of *Eclectic Horseman*. The excitement was too much to bear, so I spread it around—Carol could bring

Niji, and I called my brother, Ken, and lined him and Melissa up to come down from Maryland and take the clinic as well. Terrie even found a horse for Ken to use during the weekend so he could participate hands-on instead of just auditing. Things looked fantastic!

Two weeks ahead of the clinic, I borrowed Terrie's two-horse bumper pull trailer and put it in the pasture with Sokeri and Whipper Snapper. The only time Whipper had seen the inside of a trailer was during the episode where he tore his eye and rode to the vet hospital at Virginia Tech and back. That surely was a traumatic episode, and I figured it might take some extra time to get him used to loading. The colt still nursed and would have to accompany the mare if she was to make the clinic. I figured two weeks was plenty of time to have it all worked out, and I actually looked forward to the challenge.

The trailer was the kind with a heavy back door that swings down as a ramp. Sokeri loaded fine, she always had, but Whipper was having none of it. Curiosity immediately drew him to put a foot on the rubber-coated ramp. The faint aluminum rattle that reverberated from inside when he took a step caused his ears to prick up, and often it seemed he might just move up in there to check it out. I applied pressure and release to get more forward steps towards the inside. Patience gathered from stores I didn't even know existed were drawn upon to attempt to load that rascal. Days of creative pressure and release tactics were used to no avail. At Terrie's suggestion I even left the ramp down one day while I was away to give Whipper the opportunity to explore the strange cave-like thing on his own. The yellow snowstorm of foam padding ripped from the inside of the trailer, shredded, and strewn about a quarter acre was all the evidence needed to know he'd been two-thirds of the way in, but there was no getting him in that far again.

Anger got the better of me finally. With the deadline now nearly upon us, and me working every day to get him loaded with no more progress than a foot in the door in nearly two weeks, I barely managed to walk away from the pasture to succumb to the fit of rage that exploded from me (it was sophomoric, but the frustration finally had to vent some way and I'm still grateful I was able to walk away from the horses before being a complete idiot). More than a week of trying and trying and trying and try-ing and trying some more before trying again, all in a positive way, took its toll on me.

Partially it was a really good milestone to see just how far along I *wasn't* with horses. With a lot of success in some work with Niji and Sokeri, this brought me firmly against the reality that I expected to be able to work out the trailer loading with Whipper Snapper on my own, but couldn't. Now, just a couple of days remained, and I was no closer than when the trailer had ar-rived to getting Whipper okay with it. Carol suggested scratching plan A and as plan B leaving my two home and taking turns work-ing with Niji at the clinic: she could do the groundwork in the morning, and I could ride in the afternoon. It sounded good to me, and Niji loaded just fine!

The clinic was the 16th and 17th of April, a Saturday/Sunday deal, but we trailered Niji over a couple days before, and he set-tled into a roomy paddock with another gelding named Black-jack. On the Friday before, Carol and I went to Terrie's to check on Niji and help with some preparations. Ken and Melissa came in from Maryland and met us there. In the afternoon Bill Scott arrived with his three-horse trailer. Bill and I had spoken several times by this point, and after helping get his trailer straight I introduced myself. The conversation took right off, and I worked hard not to suck *all* the information out of the man's brain right there, leaving only an empty shell of a clinician for the others, though it really took effort. Instantly Bill seemed like a person well suited for me to learn from. He has a knack for being very articulate about horsemanship, which is great for me trying to get answers to questions with my own horses and an added bonus when trying to get some information down in article form as well.

Finally I was able to force myself to leave the conversation and the growing number of horses. Ken and I left Carol and Melissa and a bunch of others there and headed home to take care of other animals and have some fun on the farm that evening, since the rest of our time no doubt would be consumed by the clinic. The weather promised to be sunny for the weekend, a stroke of luck for this outdoor event in April in Virginia.

DAY ONE

The next morning dawned crisp, sunny, and breezy. Carol and I had a flat tire on the way over, not a great way to start out. Still, we arrived a little early, and I drank coffee with Bill and again made a concerted effort not to bogart his time, though we got to talking and covered a bunch of horse subjects even before the clinic started. There is no doubt many great clinicians aren't the best speakers. Some people learn fine from being handed plenty of rope and an open opportunity to hang themselves, which I hear is not uncommon at many clinics, but I prefer a little cerebral activity leading up to my embarrassing situations. Bill starts each day with an informal classroom gathering where he explains the day's plan and folks get to ask some questions before getting their horses. It seemed a great way to work a clinic; at least for me it was extremely helpful.

Clinics seem special worlds unto themselves. First, without the support of a clinician, it would be nearly impossible for the beginner to get so much done with a horse in two days. The clinic world is somehow isolated from the usual laws of life by some force field. In it, the links to the outside world are severed for awhile. The mind seems to know it now has an unencumbered space to focus on the one important task before it—getting better with a horse. Even time melts away, not ticking out its normal daily ration of minutes, but allowing so much more to be accomplished from sun-up to sundown.

Saturday morning, Carol entered the arena with Niji for groundwork with at least fifteen other horses, including a bay Arabian named Fable that Ken was working with. The large rectangular arena was defined by an oak board fence. It sat perched atop a hill, and the view spread over a bit of the Blue Ridge Mountains. Towards one end inside the confines of the arena, a round pen of interconnected gray metal fence panels stood set up. The range of horse folks and horses was quite broad. Looking over the fairly crowded arena, I noticed that out of all the participants, Ken and I were the only men. Thoroughbreds, Quarter Horses, an Appaloosa, Arabians, and even a Chincoteague pony moved about on their leads. The hard, white crushed stone footing crunched slightly under hoofs and boots, and before long produced a fine dust that covered every surface and gave us all a peculiar gray hue. In many of the pictures developed later, it looked deceptively like puffy soft snow around our feet.

I took notes on many of the points Bill made and did my best to snap some decent pictures with Carol's camera (it's always

Carol practicing groundwork with Niji on day one.

pretty evident she's the photographer, not me). Not even two minutes passed before many evident respect issues between horses and their people overshadowed the nuts and bolts of the basic groundwork exercise everyone began working on. Bill chose Niji right then to give an example of how to overcome them.

Bill took the lead rope from Carol and showed some basic groundwork exercises with Niji. These were mostly related to defining one's space. In particular, he worked on moving Niji's front end around. Niji was pretty rude with his head, and Bill showed how he defines his space by projecting a personal bubble with his posture and, when needed, his arms. Then he asked the horse to move the front quarters around.

At first, Bill actually had to move up against Niji's neck and shoulder, since the horse didn't yield to Bill's space. So Bill put his arms up, walked towards Niji's front, made contact with his shoulder with one forearm and his jaw with the other hand, and when Niji stonewalled, he bumped on the horse's jaw with his hand. The result was Niji got the message, and the instant he yielded, Bill released the pressure and then built on that foundation. Within a few minutes, Niji yielded to Bill's human space zone just fine and had improved in general disposition as well. Carol took back a tuned-up Niji and went through many exercises with far greater ease than before. Bill got another horse with similar issues and began showing again what he had just done with Niji, as well as getting the gelding to back by shaking the lead rope, which turned out to be a bit challenging at first.

The whole morning was spent on groundwork like this. Bill rode around on his horse, Abe, keeping an eye on the class from that high vantage point and providing guidance to all, at the level each needed. Every so often he dismounted to show an exercise with someone's horse. As a result, everyone improved, and the difference from the onlookers' position sitting on the fence gazing out over the arena from just a few hours before was quite staggering—motions were much more fluid, and many of the rough edges had softened. A great deal of willingness appeared in the horses throughout the arena. There are a hundred great examples of progress to share from just that one session, but suffice it to say that an experienced clinician with talent sees in two seconds where both horse and handler are individually and in their relationship. With some sound advice and hands-on, up-close examples, progress often is quick to materialize. By the time lunch rolled around, it seemed more like a whole day's worth of work already had transpired. My head steadily lost track of all the information just processed, and by the time I sat down to eat with everyone I just gave up trying to hold on to it and began enjoying the moment and the break.

After lunch with Carol, Ken, Melissa, and several other friends, I saddled up Niji by his paddock without any trouble. Now I'd get to ride, while Carol went about the business of taking photos. The excitement had built up in me over the morning (not to mention the weeks leading up to the clinic). I'm a hands-on person, and all that observing had me completely stoked to work with a horse. Horses and humans preparing for the afternoon session were moving everywhere, displaying further evidence of a great variety of riding styles: English and Western saddles, snaffle bits and rope halters, half chaps and shotgun chaps, helmets, reatas tied to saddles, and even a crop or two. I could have spent a couple hours just going around and asking about tack, especially Bill's really nice handmade hackamore—head gear I had read about but never seen in person before. As everyone gravitated towards the arena, Niji and I did also.

The crowd congregated in the arena and began to mount. I put my foot in the stirrup, tipped Niji's head towards me, and gave him the "Okay, I'm hopping up now" look. He stood still. But, when I hopped up to lay my belly across the saddle for the sack-of-potatoes position, he bolted out from under me. The lead rope was in my hand and I held it, easily bringing him back around, but after that simple attempt to get in the saddle, the gelding was unapproachable. It was impossible even to get near Niji's side to think about mounting. This was a new development, and quite a surprise. I couldn't even walk along his side and stand near the saddle, let alone try to get that first foot in the stirrup.

We danced around. My previous experience with Sokeri left me certain that if they move when you go to mount, *don't get on!* So around we went with me not getting on until Bill was ready to start the riding session and came over and said politely, "Why don't you take him in the round pen for awhile." So I did.

Fable gave Ken trouble as well, so the only two riders confined to the round pen and *not* riding their saddled horses were the Moates brothers, the only two men there. Neither of us cared about that, though; we just worked hard to try and get things going better with those horses.

Niji and I tried to sort out the mounting issue. I wracked my brains to find the answer. I went back to circling him a bunch in each direction, backing him, flexing his neck, all the stuff we had been doing earlier. It all went fine and he regained confidence, but the second he sensed my intention to go for that stirrup he danced off. It was a pretty severe concern on his part, and it did not melt away. I figured it had to do with those previous wrecks at home. Regardless, there were no signs whatever of improvement on our side of the round corral.

Then it occurred to me to use the rope differently. Approaching the gelding's middle and rear in any way with my arms or body was impossible at this point, so desensitizing him by rubbing him in those areas or rubbing the stirrups along his sides was not going to happen. So, I took the end of my lead rope and quickly tossed it up across his back and the saddle. It was worrisome to him at first, but he had been desensitized to it before as it is a basic maneuver in the Parelli play, so he didn't completely lose his cool. I dragged it across his back and onto the ground, then tossed again. I alternated between letting it land on the leather of the saddle and on his rump behind the cantle. Doing this for awhile got him relaxing to some stimulus in that area of his body pretty well. Working this way allowed me to hold the lead to avoid him walking off, keep my body near his head in a less threatening position than walking towards his midsection had been, and still get some sensation going to the problem places on his body.

These positive results showed the first real progress of the hours spent in the round pen. After I tossed the rope across his back and rump for awhile, he finally really relaxed for it, even licking and chewing contently. This allowed me to slowly work my way to rubbing along his sides, back, and butt with my hands. After awhile, he even stood for me to put my foot in the stirrup. Of course the next step was to hop up to the sack-of-potatoes position. I got as far along as that first foiled attempted mount—foot in the stirrup while he stood and starting to pull myself up—but with the exact same results: he took off and was unapproachable along his sides afterwards. Every so often a word from the arena loudspeaker would break into my concentrated mind: "lead change," "trot," and such, which made me just shake my head. I certainly had envisioned the clinic being much different than this. That exuberance to get hands-on with a horse had taken on a very different reality than I'd envisioned, but I kept at it even as fatigue began to grind away at me.

The afternoon began to give way to evening, and the riders were finishing up. I was mentally and physically fried, and I'm sure Niji was even more so. Bill came over and said, "I was watching you, and you were getting some things worked out there. Tomorrow after lunch we'll put him in the round pen and see what we can do."

That made me feel better. Any progress I had made felt small. Honestly, it felt more like I had caused problems that day rather than worked through anything, but Bill's words were encouraging. Plus, I was *really* curious to see this experienced horseman work Niji in the round pen.

For a complete change of pace, Bill taught a roping workshop after the horses were put away for the day. He brought out a plastic steer head and stuck it in a bale of hay, and we all tried to follow how to handle the stiff ranching-type ropes and rope it. It was a blast! Then came dark and a surprise birthday party for Terrie. It was a never-ending day, but day two finally did arrive . . . .

DAY TWO

The following morning started with a longer classroom session, since there were lots of questions relating to the previous day's work. The morning session in the arena was again spent on groundwork. I ended up taking the morning session with Niji this time, since Carol wanted to get more photos and I'd been working on those serious mounting problems at the end of the previous day.

Niji was easygoing that brisk, sunny morning, acing all the groundwork and putting a smile on my face. I felt more confident with my horse-handling skills after the intensive isolated round pen episode. Terrie felt bad that the horse she had lined up for Ken was so difficult, and gave him her horse, Spirit, who is an absolute dream, to work with that morning. Then we had lunch, and afterwards Bill stuck to his suggestion from the day before and we walked with Niji up to the round pen to work out the mounting kinks.

Bill took a look at the saddle I'd had on him the day before, suspicious that perhaps Niji's problem might be related to its fit. He didn't like the looks of the cheap saddle and suggested I switch over to Carol's Big Horn roping saddle, which we also had brought. I only had one cinch, and I had made the billet from a new piece of belt leather. I pulled this rigging off the little saddle and outfitted the heavy one with it, then carried it over and placed it on the ground outside the round pen.

The differences between Niji's mounting issues and Sokeri's are pretty broad. Sokeri wasn't frightened. She, for whatever reason in her horse mind, wasn't accepting me. I had to communicate to her through pressure and release, and through persistence, that I would insist on the same consideration every time I went to get on. It would have been great if I could have made her think standing still for mounting was *her* idea, but I didn't figure that out. After awhile, with good-natured perseverance, we got it sorted out. Niji, on the other hand, had several consecutive bad experiences involving me coming off his back and verged on panic when I tried to mount. This situation involved a higher level of energy, with the potential for danger much greater than with Sokeri. I think Niji was scared for both of us and was not allowing me to take the lead. With him, I would have to establish a whole new level in our relationship, as well as communicate better, work through desensitizing him to my getting on him, and overcome my own fears, which also grew every time he bolted and I went flying off. Putting aside those fears and being assertive were essential. I would have to do whatever it took to build his confidence and be able to get on when the time was right. I figured some of this out on my own as we approached the round pen with Niji.

Bill had me put the sorrel gelding in the round pen and re-move the rope halter. By this time a crowd had gathered. Nearly everyone had heard Bill was going to work Niji in the round pen and stood close by, eyes focused intently on us. Bill stood in the middle, decked out in a straw cowboy hat and leather shotgun chaps with a coiled rope in hand. I retreated out the gate with the halter and lead rope and then leaned on the fence to watch, near Carol with her camera, Ken, and his wife Melissa with her camera. You'd have thought it was the feature act at the rodeo—the top-rated bull taking on the top-rated bull rider—the way the crowd huddled around.

Niji moved around the pen looking out at some other horses in a field close by. "Notice how this horse isn't paying attention to me?" Bill said closely observing him. "I don't want that. I want him to look to me, not out there."

Bill sorted the coils of his rope between his hands, and then, with them evenly divided, he smacked the left set against his chaps and moved towards Niji. The horse changed his focus onto Bill and started moving around the pen. Bill pushed him to trot and after several minutes changed his body position by stepping somewhat in front of the moving horse, turning slightly, and then backing away. Niji stopped and turned towards him.

"Now I'll offer him a good deal," the cowboy explained and stepped towards the horse with an arm extended to stroke him on the nose. As he approached, it seemed that Niji would stay fo-cused on him. However, at the last second the gelding turned his head and attention elsewhere. Bill backed up and lowered the arm, asking again for his focus. When it didn't return, he smacked the rope on the chaps again, and Niji was on his way around the corral.

"I offered him a good deal, and he didn't take it," the horse-man explained from the middle of the pen, horse scooting around the edge right by the fence. "He could choose to either focus on me and stand or not, but if he doesn't, he's made the choice to move his feet, so I send him around again like this. Soon he'll get it." Sure enough it wasn't long before Niji was completely focused on Bill. With both eyes fixed on the cowboy, Niji got some comforting strokes on the nose. Then, Bill could walk any-where in that pen and Niji would keep his eyes right on him and even follow him around to stay close.

At Bill's request, I brought in the saddle and blanket. He took the blanket and rubbed it all over the gelding's neck, back, and butt to desensitize him to it. Then he showed how he likes to put on a saddle by holding it in one arm and swinging it up and gen-tly into place on the horse. Niji didn't seem to be troubled by any of this. Bill noticed the back cinch on the saddle and had me re-move it; there was nothing connecting it to the front cinch which would let it move a lot, and he didn't want anything extra flop-ping around under the gelding to worry him. I cinched him up.

Bill Scott offering Niji "a good deal."

Then, to my surprise, Bill said to me, "All right, get your rope, get in here, and send him around the pen." So I did. By this time the whole clinic group was there watching intently, and I think other people even had materialized from somewhere. It seemed like fifty people must have been gazing on the spectacle of me entering the round pen at this point.

I got Niji walking, then trotting, by copying what I had just seen Bill do with the coiled up rope. Then with guidance from the cowboy's voice amplified through the PA system, I upped my energy and tossed the tail of my halter rope towards the horse and got him to transition up to a canter. It took a good deal of energy to keep him there, as well as more rope tossing and me running a smaller circle within his larger circle. It was dizzying, and the rest of the world melted away into a blur except for a clear view of Niji's body and Bill's voice in my ear. We ran until I was parched and nearly spent. Then, when I backed off the pressure and turned slightly to get Niji to "hook on" and pay attention to me, my timing was off. I did manage to get his undivided attention, for which he was awarded rest and a nose stroking (and me a bottle of water), but as my timing was a little late, I did not draw him in towards me the way Bill had done.

The idea here is to establish yourself in the mind of the horse as the lead horse. Amongst horses, whoever controls the feet of the other is leader (Mark Rashid calls another type of herd leader the "passive leader," which I'm learning is a little different, but here we discuss the typical alpha leader scenario). Horses communicate largely through body language, and whoever moves the others is respected. In this setting, we established that Niji could choose either to respect me with his attention or not, but I controlled whether he moved or not.

After a bit of this, he quickly learned it was a much better deal to respect me and gain some stillness. Once established, this respect can carry over into other parts of the horse-human relationship, which was the hope here.

Next Bill had me put on the halter and lead rope and do an exercise called "circling up." This is where you start out standing beside your horse's shoulder looking towards his butt, holding the rope in the hand closest to him with about three feet of slack in the rope, and then walk towards his rear end. The horse should start to move his rear away from you (frequently called disengaging or untracking the hindquarters) and begin to move in a circle. You keep this up so he gets moving nicely and then reach up with the other hand, grab the rope closer to the halter, then bring that hand with its grip on the rope down to your hip opposite the horse and place the free hand closest to the horse on his withers. The horse should transition from circling to a stop with his head flexed nicely in your direction. The instant this is happening, you release the pressure on the rope for reward. I did this multiple times in both directions.

And thus, Niji was prepared for the moment of mounting without stepping off (or I should say bolting, in his case). With everyone's eyes on us, I went through the basic preflight steps: checked the cinch for tightness and stood at his shoulder, facing the back of the horse. With my near hand, I grabbed the near rein and a handful of mane; I turned the stirrup and placed the foot in it (being careful, as Bill pointed out, not to poke him in the side with the toe of my boot); I held the back of the saddle with my other hand and gave the "Okay, I'm getting on now" look. Then I stepped up and laid across the saddle in the sack-of-potatoes position—he stood still! "Rub him, rub him!" Bill

Making some progress.

reminded me as I lay there soaking in the awesome reality. Then I hopped down, moved him to a new spot, tried again, and had the same fantastic results.

After getting us both confident with the stepping-up phase of getting on, I went ahead and carefully threw my leg over and was able to sit on him to the applause and big smiles of the crowd. It was a huge moment. Melissa snapped the picture at the beginning of this chapter right then as I rubbed and praised him. The fulfillment of seeing that much work pay off, and being able to work through a difficult problem with someone like Bill, who really knows what he is doing, is profound. Bill stressed later how much having a human work through a problem in a good way means to the horse. His horse's-view perspective startled me several times that weekend and began to change the way I viewed situations with horses. I began to see more deeply the level of confidence a horse can gain in a person and just how much we can be there for the horse.

Now that mounting was an option, I tied the long lead rope around like a mecate type of rein to his rope halter and got in the saddle. Once I was on Niji, he responded to all my requests like a champion. He backed, moved fore- and hindquarters, walked wherever I asked in the round pen, and did so in a perfectly calm frame of mind.

Ken and Melissa had to leave for the long drive back to Maryland then, and they had actually stayed longer than planned to watch this special round corral session with Niji. I dismounted and we said our good-byes. They were really pleased to have stayed to witness such a big breakthrough, and figured, as did I, next we'd be riding with the group that afternoon.

They took off and I got back in the round pen and had no trouble getting on Niji and riding him around again. Another participant wanted to use the round pen to tune up her horse before riding, so I went ahead and rode Niji out into the arena. Just outside the round pen gate I stopped him. We turned this way and that, and walked a little way one direction and then the other. He was perfect, and I was relaxing into the great moment. I even began to realize how different his motions were compared to Sokeri's—with Niji's Quarter Horse/Arabian body it was easier to feel his movements, whereas the Walking Horse was so fluid it was more difficult to know where her legs were from the saddle.

Then it happened.

I suppose Bill was trying to get everyone's attention to start the riding session. He was on Abe about ten feet away from Niji and me. The arena again was packed with horses and riders all mounted. Bill whistled. His microphone picked it up and the PA amplified it. Niji bolted.

I remember grabbing the left rein that went to the rope halter and pulling for the one-rein stop. I also remember deciding to ride this out rather than bailing when Niji didn't bend. I remember Niji galloping for all he was worth in a straight line the length of the arena, straight for the oak board fence at one end. I remember thinking about oak, and how strong it really is, and just what might happen to a horse that runs right into a fence constructed from it.

I wasn't sure exactly what happened next. The twenty eyewitness accounts I heard later, including Bill's, say that I stuck in there, and at the last second before Niji crashed into the fence, he turned in the direction of the rein I'd been pulling on and stopped. If you look at that picture from a few minutes before, notice the billet. That's the one I made from a belt. It ripped like tissue paper and broke. I stayed in the saddle, but the saddle came off the horse. I rode that saddle a hundred miles an hour down into the stone dust, along the ground, and under the bottom oak fence board right between two posts like a human hockey puck in a goal.

If I had been two inches in any other direction than where I ended up, I'd have been really hurt, or perhaps even killed. Instead, I bloodied up my left forearm and my hip and trashed the Big Horn, but was okay. I got up, dusted off, and there stood Niji right by the fence where I'd gone under, with a face that looked as if to say, *Hey . . . you okay? What you doing down there?*

The whole thing was pretty upsetting to everyone. I think folks realized I was okay only after I got up and borrowed another saddle to start over again with Niji in the round pen. Absolute determination welled in me to get back on Niji, as I could not leave things with him on such a horrible note after such a great clinic with so many breakthroughs.

Everyone again rode their horses in the arena, learning all kinds of great fancy stuff, while I hobbled around, becoming increasingly sore, with Niji in our isolated round corral world. This time, however, I had more tools in my groundwork toolbox. In a couple of hours, things were starting to look good with Niji. I got to mounting and sitting on him, a huge relief after another big wreck on him. Then we got back to riding around in there and getting along really nicely.

At the end of the day, after all but Bill and Abe and a couple others had left the arena, I rode Niji out of the round pen. "Don't whistle or make any sudden sounds!" I half-joked with Bill. We discussed the turn of events as I easily rode the gelding all over that arena without trouble. When I told Bill about the homemade billet, he explained that belts and billets are made from different types of leather, and he believed if it hadn't been for the equipment failure that Niji would have stopped and I'd have stayed on.

I went out directly and bought all new rigging for the saddle.

CHAPTER TWELVE

HORSES NEVER LIE

A VISION CLEARLY BRANDED ITSELF into the gray matter of my brain—Carol and I in saddles walking the horses lazily, sunshine warming our faces as we soak in the silence of the mountains, hearing the faint trickling of the Little River in the distance. This daydream seemed even more tangible, since Sokeri and I already had ridden the route together several times now. Even the mountain winter obliged by providing regular bi-weekly respites from snow and sub-zero temperatures with gorgeous sunny days, the mercury stretching well above sixty. But my vision included Carol on Niji; this would be the first part of the vision to change.

Niji was too inexperienced to attempt riding out in the world. The gelding's disposition was fantastic, and he was moving along well with the groundwork—he even stood fine for saddling and mounting at that point—but he had been ridden only a few times. Carol's health had kept her from doing much with Niji lately, and I gladly picked up the slack. The last ride had been both the best and the worst. The best because, as my communication in the saddle had improved by riding Sokeri, I was able to ask and get results with him like never before. He matter-of-factly responded to the basic rein and leg cues for moving the front and hindquarters, as well as stepping forwards and back. It was thrilling! The worst because my ecstatic, overconfident moment brought on a bit of oversight. The horses here are moved at times to different pastures for various reasons, and Niji lately had been alone at the house paddock for a few weeks to make it easy for Carol to have a little time with him. I decided to ride him slowly up the farm road to the upper pasture where the other two horses were to give them some time together. The joy of ambling along in the saddle down our road through the forest lasted a couple hundred feet; then, without warning, the Arab/Quarter Horse cross bolted, leaving me crumpled up on the gravel and snapped back to the reality of my poor judgment. *Of course* I thought staring up at the sky and slowly testing to see if any parts of me were broken, *if I was a horse in this situation, I'd make a run for the others in a bigger pasture too.* After such a great, groundbreaking ride just before, the mistake was especially painful. We could not risk Carol taking such a spill. Niji needed more time to be safe to mount outside the round pen. But the image of that trail ride persisted, and a plan B horse began to develop in my mind: Spirit!

Spirit is one of those horses whose statue belongs towering before the entrance to the all-time-greatest-horse hall of fame. This twenty-ish bay Arabian gelding, with a lightning bolt blaze running from poll to nose, is the essence of dependable. He was the perfect choice for Carol in plan B. Spirit's person is Terrie Wood, the natural horse trainer, barefoot trimmer, and now closest of friends, who got us started on the natural horse path.

Quite a bit earlier when Niji, Soke, and I were learning some basic groundwork, it occurred to me I had no reference for where we were heading with this training. Sokeri even came to the farm already "broke" and could theoretically be ridden, but I wasn't ready to hop on her and go; besides, I had seen the way she had been handled and wanted to start from the ground up with this other way with horses.

Videos and books can help some, but there is a huge difference between book/video knowledge and experience. This is where artificiality meets reality, where speaking and writing max out their potential and become meaningless without feeling the tangible objects that they attempt to reference. And, even if I could get the basic ideas down about how to ride a horse from such media, I was still dealing with live horses—conscious beings with minds and temperaments of their own. Lack of experience was truly a disadvantage.

So one nice Saturday morning, back in the summer, I drove over to Terrie's farm, and she put a saddle pad and a rope halter with a mecate rein rig on Spirit. In the outdoor arena, with its perfectly level stone-dust footing and board fence defining the rectangular area, I would get my first taste of the ride and feel of a natural horse. Spirit scared me at first, standing there quietly as I slid on from the fence and patiently waiting for me to ask him to do something. After about thirty seconds, with Terrie explaining how to work the reins and the rest of my body, the real world melted away and it was just Spirit and I.

The way Terrie acquainted me with the reins on Spirit I now know was straight Parelli. Again, it seems the Parellis have a really good way to introduce people to various stages of working with horses. First, I learned that when I let go of the reins and let them set on Spirit's neck, he stopped. Beginners, Terrie explained, haven't established any feel with the reins, so they can be too harsh on the bit. To try to help eliminate sudden yanks or overzealous pulls on the reins, she had me lift them with my left hand and "pump" the right rein three times with my right hand and arm before taking a hold of it about halfway, putting a little pressure on it, and having Spirit respond by bending his head in that direction, back towards my right knee, and then releasing the rein—that's lateral flexion. The multistep request allows the horse to anticipate that the beginner is about to ask for something with the rein before it happens and avoid surprises. It also makes the rider consciously prepare before putting pressure on the rein. These combine to create a smoother transition when the novice uses the reins.

I practiced it on both sides. Then, I'd pump the rein and bring it a little further than before, aiming that active rein hand toward the opposite shoulder, and add a little heel pressure on the side his head was bending toward, which moved his hindquarters away from my foot. When I released the pressure from the reins and my foot, he stopped. That was disengaging the hindquarters. We went through moving the forequarters and backing as well, and then added some simple combinations that put to the test my ability to put it all together in different ways.

The amazing thing about the ride was how natural it felt to me. I don't know if all that video had sunk in through osmosis, if I had some dormant aptitude for these exercises, or if they're just that easy, but it flowed. And riding a horse pretty far along in his natural horsemanship training had been the right thing to do—it completely ingrained in me what to head toward with my horse. I was so absorbed that the hour session accidentally became two. I was sore in my legs for days afterward, not from using them forcefully, just from using muscles that had lain dormant for so many years. Without any doubt, those two hours helped me more with getting where I needed to go with my mare than anything previous. Every time I get on a horse, I still use those basic reining skills Terrie and Spirit taught me that day.

"Terrie, would you trailer Spirit over for Carol and another horse for you and go riding with us around here?" I asked the voicemail on her cell phone. She called back in a couple of days, and we were set, in theory, for a sunny day in the not-too-distant-future.

The smoke from that trail riding picture branded in my brain still wafted around inside my head, so the excitement held up pretty well against the snow that blew in on fifty-mile-an-hour winds after that call, even though the only sun around here was in my trail riding fantasy. The snow piled up, and we hunkered down. Carol busied herself cutting and sewing quilt blocks. I practiced approach and retreat, not so much with the horses as approaching the fuel I needed in the woods with a chainsaw and retreating to warmth of the upstairs office to write.

Then, with no advance warning, the weather broke. Things warmed up, the snow melted, and the forecast called for a day in the sixties, with sunshine and no wind! "Can you come with the horses to ride *tomorrow*?" my exuberant, near-panicked voice probably shouted into the voicemail on Terrie's cell phone.

Then I waited.

Ten minutes went by. I thought of trying her again, but I knew how stupid that would be. A couple of hours went by.

With Terrie's busy schedule as a hoof trimmer and mother, I figured the window of opportunity likely would be lost to the next blizzard—perfectly understandable. I began making a mental cushion for my fall. But I'd forgotten one key aspect of this situation: we were inviting Terrie over to *ride*. She finally called back with a hearty, "Sure! I'll be there at eleven."

I bounced off the walls and did my best not to talk Carol to death about it. The next morning was crisp and blue skied, just like my vision. Our horses were in an upper pasture some distance from the house. Terrie would trailer hers to the house. I decided to go and saddle up Sokeri early and ride her to the house so she would be ready to go and already away from Whipper Snapper and Niji, thereby causing less disruption with the new horses around.

The sun on their fuzzy winter coats warmed them that morning to complete tranquility. All three stood, each with a rear leg cocked, in a sun coma when I got up there around eleven. Saddling up Soke went with ease, and I then rode her down the farm road and over to the house just fine. Soke and I had been going for rides away from the other two for several weeks now in preparation. Even the still-nursing colt was fine when the mare was absent for an hour at a time, perhaps a testament to Niji's babysitting skills.

Just as the house came into sight, we saw Terrie's green F-250 pickup and gray two-horse trailer driving down another farm

Things started out just fine that day.

road toward the house from the other side. Sokeri changed. I *felt* the change. The sensation was not just in her body—which did stiffen, her head raised with ears focusing on the trailer—but was also in the energy field around her, which included me. She became electric, like the air just before a storm. I noticed it, but attributed it to the excitement and curiosity of new horses coming onto the farm.

Terrie parked, Carol came out to greet her, and I stopped close to the rear of the trailer with Sokeri so she could have a look at the other horses. The electricity around her remained, but she listened to me pretty well anyway. I rode her a couple hundred feet away and tied her to a locust rail fence.

Spirit was in the trailer with Woody, a black-and-white paint Chincoteague pony who was about as big as any pony could be at 14 hands and fat enough that it's easy to see the reference when Terrie calls him her Orca. Woody was four, and this was his first excursion off the farm and his first real trail ride. Terrie brought him to get started in this life of traveling out to new places that lay before him and test how the foundation training they'd been working on was really setting with him. She dropped the trailer ramp and butt chain, lightly lifted a few hairs from his tail, and he backed out calmly in response to that tiny bit of pressure and looked around. Spirit came out likewise. Carol and Terrie brushed and tacked these two, then mounted up.

Bubbling with exuberance at this point, I untied Sokeri and walked her to the road. I circled her each direction, checked the cinch, grabbed hold of the near rein with a handful of mane, and put my foot in the stirrup. Sokeri began moving away from me. *Oh no!* I thought. *Come on, we've worked on this. We're past this stepping-off thing. Just stand like you should.*

No deal. We practiced this disengage-the-hindquarter dance for several minutes. Terrie and Carol sat there in their saddles chatting pleasantly as I began to stress out and tried to keep from showing it. Finally I broke a cardinal rule and got into that saddle anyway, although the mare was definitely not okay with the situation. With all the progress of recent weeks, I just desperately wanted to have this moment. I really hoped that once in the saddle, the horse and I would get back to the type of enjoyable, easygoing ride of recent days. I knew better, even back then, and I didn't know why she was getting so wound-up. But hopes, dreams, and expectations die hard. And horses never, ever lie to you.

Right from the start, Sokeri was weirded out. I can only speculate that the new horses bothered her, or perhaps the trailer reminded her of the last time one showed up—when she and Whipper went to the Virginia Tech Vet Hospital for his emergency eye surgery. Whatever the reason, the result was that she would stop and go, then GO! I had to use the one-rein stop on her over and over again—which was almost never necessary on our solitary rides anymore—just in the first several hundred feet of the ride. Spirit and Woody walked along slowly, seemingly content, even though visiting a place unfamiliar to them.

After much effort on my part trying to patch my mare's emotions back together, and with my own becoming increasingly untethered, we approached the upper field where Niji and Whipper Snapper trotted around, tails flagged, voicing their interest in the newcomers. Spirit and Woody walked by just like pros, turning their heads calmly as if to say, *Hey guys.* Soke kept up the dance, and once past the upper field and into the narrow gauntlet of a road defined on either side by newly strung barbed wire, she tangoed her butt right into a multiflora rose bush. A ten-foot-long thorny branch became tangled in her tail and started swinging around her like a barbed weapon in our constant one-rein-stop circles.

That was it. I dismounted. As calmly as I could manage with my increasingly tense body, I began the challenging process of untangling Sokeri's tail, nearly strand by strand, from the sticker bush from hell. Carol and Terrie had been following Sokeri and me to this point. Here they went on ahead, slowly walking their horses, chatting, laughing, and every so often glancing back to see where we were in the course of things. Then Soke and I replayed the earlier tape of, "When not to mount your horse because she won't stand still." I finally got so dizzy from spinning around that I went ahead and walked Sokeri down the lane to get a little farther away from Whip and Niji and headed in another direction where we love to ride.

Two hundred feet later, after much stroking and soft words, to Sokeri's credit, she finally allowed me to hop up in the saddle while she stood. Open fields and a loamy ten-acre stretch down by the river with the mountains rising up on the far side spread out before us now. Hope for that blissful ride swelled in my chest again. *Maybe if we just get down by the river, she'll mellow out*, I thought. The main lessons of that day would turn out to be: horses don't snap out of such troubles quickly, and expectations are a human contrivance guaranteed to ensure disappointments.

Sokeri got worse. She would manage a few steps, then I'd feel the surge forward. A one-rein stop was the only thing dissuading her from just taking off. She was ready to gallop full speed, somewhere, anywhere—she was just about to jump out of her skin. Instead of tiring, or listening to me, or falling in with the others, she got worse. Finally, she would hardly take a single step at a walk, and there were fewer than three feet between one-rein stops. It was as if she was in a constant and unabating panic. Her flight instinct had completely consumed her thought processes. She wanted to get to "safety," I guessed, which I figured was with the others at home base.

Her near-bolting starts were now peppered with the most nervous bouts of snatching mouthfuls of grass I'd ever seen in a horse. *My* stomach began to knot up from the stress of it—and as for her, all the neck stroking, calm words, and lateral flexions at what standstills we could manage did no good. Finally, just as we got to the river, I accepted reality, dismounted, and decided to walk her back home. The stress in us wasn't subsiding (at this point we really were verging on meltdown, which was another first for me), and there was no need to continue making us both crazy. Terrie later would say, "You stayed on her longer than I would have, and it showed good judgment for her and for your safety to be willing to get off and walk her finally. A lot of people wouldn't have done that." Coming from a natural horse person I have great respect for, that made me feel a little better.

So back to the upper field we walked, with Carol and Terrie ambling along comfortably behind us on Spirit and Woody. I kept wondering if this was what is called "herdbound," where horses can act like Soke did because they want so strongly to be back with their buddies at home. The really odd thing about that theory was that she hadn't acted this way when we rode to these very places alone, just the two of us. And why wouldn't being with these two other horses *help* with that problem? Also, she had started freaking out as we headed from the house *in the direction of Niji and Whipper and home base* at first. It was a total mystery to me. I even checked her saddle for some unseen pine cone or pricker bush that might accidentally have gotten under the saddle blanket and caused discomfort, but there was nothing, not even a burr.

She settled down when I got her back in with her regular crew in the upper pasture. I wondered about the wisdom of giving in to her behavior, but her actions were so severe and persistent, and escalating for that matter, that I really feared for her well-being. Given that, I knew in my gut it was the right thing to do. Besides, the future was open to work through problems with her. My trail ride fantasy could come another day.

Woody, in contrast, did well with his first big adventure, but not without adding some badly needed comic relief. Woody, it seems, is scared of rocks. Terrie's place doesn't have the rock outcroppings we have here. The gelding would up his energy as they approached good-sized rocks (which were everywhere), flare his nostrils, cautiously sneak up on them, and even snort.

"Wood-eee!" Terrie exclaimed, "I can't believe you're afraid of *rocks*! How silly!" She spent plenty of time introducing him to these strange alien creatures, but for all her work, he remained dubious.

Carol and Spirit, who took superb care of her, just enjoyed the sunny day to the fullest. After several months of being inside, laid up recuperating from a bout of surgery in late November, it was a huge consolation to me that at least she got to get out and enjoy the day on a horse.

Winter returned the next day. I bundled up, took the rope halter and lead rope with a deep breath, and went to the round pen with Sokeri.

CHAPTER THIRTEEN

OLD BLUE EYES

THE EARLY EXPERIENCES I HAD with horses involved only natural horsemanship. Sometimes, when I was lucky, I was able to observe experienced folks like Terrie using these methods with their horses in person. Other times I practiced the pressure and release methods alone with our horses. Often I just soaked in natural horsemanship books and videos, trying to get a good mental grip on the basics and being spellbound by the more complicated stuff like bridleless riding.

Before long, though, through a fairly odd series of events, an opportunity arose for me to visit a mainstream cutting horse operation firsthand. It is easy to pick up attitudes when learning something new, and I already was keenly aware of an attitude in the natural horsemanship movement against horsemanship not officially sanctioned "natural." Fortunately, my all-consuming love for horses overwhelmed my preconceived notions. I hadn't lost sight of the fact that I was a complete novice, natural or not, and therefore had no right to judge anyone else. Especially a successful horseman, mainstream or not. So, desperate to learn more about horses, I jumped at the opportunity to see a renowned trainer in action. The seed for this encounter, oddly enough, had been planted years before.

At the end of each summer for the past five years, I've driven a truck and trailer down to Fletcher, North Carolina, outside of Asheville, to the agricultural center there. Although the facility is a major equestrian center for the area, it's not horses I've hauled down, but rather solar panels, energy efficient appliances, and copies of my book on hydraulic ram pumps. I make this trip to help out my friend, Bryan Walsh, who owns a renewable energy contracting company called Solar Connexion. We run his massive booth each year at the Southern Energy and Environment Expo. The expo is set up in the main indoor arena, and most of the other facilities, such as the livestock stalls and smaller arenas, lay dormant during the three-day event.

One evening in the second year as I stood, exhausted and unable to sleep at the camping spot sandwiched right between a busy interstate and the main airport for the region, I noticed some horse activity across the parking lot in a covered arena with open sides. An announcer on a loudspeaker was occasionally audible over the constant drone of eighteen-wheelers and the intermittent roar of jets. I could just make out the lowing of young cattle, as well. Intrigued, I decided to go check it out.

I had no idea what I was watching, but it was a blast! The cows in the pen wore numbers from 0 to 9. The announcer called a number apparently drawn at random over the loudspeaker, and the clock began to count down. A rider then walked his horse into the herd of yearlings and worked to separate the cow with that number. Once isolated, two hold-back riders tried to keep that cow at one end of the arena, while the main cutter returned to the herd and attempted to single out the next one in numerical order. The process progressed this way through all ten cows while racing against the clock. If a cut cow made a break for it and slipped past the hold-back crew back to the herd, the clock stopped and the riders were disqualified. Similarly, if an un-cut cow whose number was out of sequence ran through to join the cut cows, the team's run was over. This went on all night. I figured this was cutting and filed the experience away in my brain as supercool but completely unrelated to my life, which in no way included horses at that time.

Three years passed before Niji showed up. As my obsession with equines snowballed and I began to get better with them, the event from that sleepless night in Fletcher bubbled to the surface of my brain. Carol and I, living deep in the mountains, keep an eye out for opportunities to get away. I began to hunt for cutting competitions in the area.

I had no luck. It seemed that there were few Western competitions in Virginia, at least not that I could find online or in regional magazines. Months earlier, a friend had clipped an article from the local paper and given it to me about a woman who had bred a cutting horse and sold it for a handsome sum. In other parts of the country it may not seem like a big deal, but here in the English riding Mecca of Virginia it was newsworthy. As I re-read the article, which amazingly I located in the piles of papers in my office, it began to sink in that serious Western riders, train-ers, and horses weren't particularly prevalent in the mid-Atlantic. The article mentioned a trainer in a small town about an hour from our home who had trained the cutting horse from the arti-cle and listed a phone number for a group called the Appalachian Cutting Horse Association.

One Saturday night about nine o'clock I finally got around to calling. The live voice on the other end startled me; I had ex-pected a recorded message on a machine. It turned out that it was a cell phone number, and the fellow on the other end was Tracy Barton—the trainer from the article. He was driving back from a cutting horse competition out of state.

At the time I knew nothing of Tracy (or cutting, for that mat-ter, as my confusion between it and team penning from the Fletcher event will be obvious to the experienced), and I stum-bled through a conversation explaining I was just a person inter-ested in cutting from a few counties over. To my surprise, rather than quickly trying to get rid of my random call, in his no-doubt exhausted state he took time to speak with me and even invited me down to see his facility. Thrilled at the opportunity, I got Carol and her camera together, and we drove down to visit his training operation, Circle TTB Cutting Horses, within a week.

Later, reflecting on that first conversation, it makes me chuckle how completely clueless I was. Tracy Barton, as I soon learned, is one of the winningest riders in the cutting business. His twenty-eight Congress titles are the most of any rider in history. He has been in the top ten world rankings three times and is one of only three riders east of the Mississippi to be inducted into the National Cutting Horse Association Hall of Fame (an accolade that, at the very least, requires a rider to have won over a million dollars).

When I first called Tracy, I was just barely getting started with horses. Natural horsemanship was all I knew, and my heart was completely swept up in its priority for gentle means of working with horses. From the very beginning of this journey, a message clearly shone between the lines (and was stated in black and white many times as well) that natural horsemanship is a shift *away* from the heavy-handed and even brutal methods often seen in the traditional horse world. Inherent in all the natural horsemanship devotees I came into contact with was the underlying presence of this counter position, the sense of overcoming an evil. "You won't be able to ride with people who don't work with their horses this way," the warnings came. "They either give you too much grief, or you can't stand how they handle their horses." Certainly this perception is a result of the thrust of the natural horsemanship movement to bring about change to many long and widely accepted training methods that are at the least inefficient and at the worst downright damaging to the horse and just plain cruel.

It is true that the natural horsemanship movement is a shift in consciousness away from what might be called "mainstream horsemanship"—but, as is often the case, I came to realize we get into trouble when we start lumping things wholesale into categories. Any time you get a group of humans together who rally around an idea, there seems to be a natural tendency to develop an "us versus them" attitude by default. It is easy to fall into the trap—you like one idea and have good success with one group, so you naturally develop an attitude against another, sometimes without even knowing anything about the other. I made a conscious decision to fight to avoid that pitfall. It became my goal to try to observe objectively at the TTB, without bringing along the baggage of preconceived notions. I realized that for me, such traps could manifest not only as stigmas against mainstream training methods, but also between the various types of natural horsemanship trainers themselves as well. This controversy played in my head even before I went to Tracy's, and I braced for some impending inner conflict.

Even before riding down to see Tracy, I decided it was best if I just completely avoided discussing the topic of natural horsemanship with him. For someone who talked about the subject constantly, it would be really tough, especially around such a renowned horseman. I would have loved to get his take on the subject anyway, even if it was negative. I was motivated, however, by the very real possibility of being stigmatized by *him*. I wanted *every* opportunity to learn from talented horse folk, regardless of their background. The option to turn and walk away if what I saw became unbearable always existed, but if someone chose to categorize me and reject me wholesale because of my association with natural horsemanship, there would be little I could do. A simple invitation to see some horse training had really become this political in my mind.

I suspected that natural horse people didn't corner the market on being skilled with horses. The truth underlying my attitude was that it was clear (even to me) that I knew almost nothing about horses, and I would do almost anything to get better with them. So I went down to the TTB, kept my mouth shut except to ask questions, and began what has become one of the greatest learning experiences I've had with horses.

Anything equine magnifies the energy level of an encounter for me. Driving down, I kept searching for images in my imagination of just what this experience would be like, and I was pretty amped up about it. Perhaps the extra intensity was simply a foreshadowing of the opportunity that lay underneath the surface of that first meeting. Whatever the reason, I was kind of tense as Carol and I pulled up to the operation.

The sight of horses relaxed me a bit. I got out of the car and walked into a long barn towards the sounds of mooing and a radio playing. Inside the large structure were fifty stalls, an office, a washing area, several aisles, and a tack room, all encircling a large, open indoor arena. All the noise came from outside, through another door at the far end of the barn. I walked that way and stepped out into the sunlight, where all the action was. Behind the barn was a large round pen, probably 150 feet in diameter—way larger than any I had seen used for training purposes—made from solid plywood panels framed in metal pipe, with a deep sand footing. An electric walker that looked a little like a carousel stood thirty feet away, with four horses, attached by their halters, walking in a slow circle. Various cattle pens with a labyrinth of gates were between the barn and round pen off to my left. Immediately to my right stood a hitching rail beside a metal rack with places for half a dozen saddles and pads, and on the side of the round corral directly ahead of me was a long set of hooks, where at least forty halters and bridles of various kinds hung. Catching me by surprise, just off to the side of the round pen in clear view of the adults atop their horses within, was another piece of equipment—a swing set complete with several kids playing.

I approached the round pen from the barn and looked over a fence panel between the gate and bridles. Just as I put my face over the top bar to get a better look at what was happening inside, a cow smashed into the panel on the other side; it didn't scare me particularly, but certainly drew the attention of those inside to my wide-eyed, unfamiliar face.

The first impression everyone has of Tracy is, "Gosh, that guy's *big*," and mine was no exception. I watched as he seemed— without effort or emotion, reins slack and hands down at the base of the mane—to just move with a stallion as the horse dug into the deep sand, low to the ground, following the moves of a young cow. That's always how it is with Tracy, I've come to realize; even looming over the cutting horses with their low centers of gravity, his large frame moves with them as they work cattle. It is a testimony to how truly fluid he is as a rider—he simply has more mass to get into synch with the horse than a smaller person. When I ride at the TTB, I have to adjust the stirrups nearly to their highest position; when Tracy gets on a horse those stirrups get moved down about a foot to their lowest position.

After finishing with that cow, he rode near me on the way to cut another from the herd. I said hello, and he said he would come out and talk to me in a minute. Carol showed up, and we watched from our ring-side position as he slowly entered the herd, singled out a cow to cut, dropped the reins, and again moved with the horse as he pushed that cow out from the herd and kept it from returning to its friends.

Before dismounting the stallion and coming over, Tracy gave directions to helpers, answered the cell phone on his belt, and spoke to clients in and out of the ring. Men and women busied themselves with various equine tasks. The whirlwind of activity

Tracy Barton training a cutting horse at the TTB.

dizzied the unfamiliar observer. I introduced myself to a few folks and helped where I could, out of self-preservation if nothing else. Tracy finally exited the round pen long enough to shake my hand and get our introductions done. We talked for a few minutes, and then he said, "You want to work?"

That day Tracy and I had a few more minutes to talk, which planted the seeds for several magazine articles that would sprout in the future, but mostly I led horses to and from stalls, washed them after their sweaty/sandy workout, took saddles on and off, and observed occasionally. Tacking and un-tacking at least fifteen horses in three hours did more to familiarize me with the process than had the whole previous year of messing around with my own guys at a slower pace and watching videos about the proper way to go about it. It isn't long under that type of repetitious workout before naturally efficient motions manifest. Quickly the mind and body—helped along by occasional advice from the more experienced—arrive at the best way to deal with the saddle rigging and cinching. There were several different kinds of saddles with various kinds of rigging, so the experience provided insight into a spectrum of equipment as well.

Differences between the natural horsemanship ways and this world abounded. There was no groundwork, for instance. Teaching a horse to lead evenly on both sides had been drilled into my awareness, but here, all leading was done in the traditional way, from the left side only. But once I looked past all that kind of stuff, Tracy's horses were extremely easy to handle and light to lead. There was easy handling everywhere I looked, and a routine that the horses knew and seemed content with. There was a flow to the training regimen, and I soaked in all I could of the experience.

The routine went like this: bring out a horse from his stall, braid his tail so it doesn't get stepped on and broken during practice, place him on the mechanical walker to warm up, fetch him from the walker and saddle him, trade out the halter for a bridle with a snaffle bit, enter the round pen and lope him in a circle to further warm up, give him to Tracy for a cutting workout (sometimes requiring a bit change), collect him afterwards, trade bridle for halter, unsaddle, take out the braid, lead the horse to the wash stall and hose him down, and finally return him to the stall. Of course, this doesn't really happen one horse at a time—there might be eight horses on the walker, three loping, Tracy on one cutting, one being washed with three others tied up waiting for a turn in the wash stall, the farrier working on shoes, and the vet checking on others, all at once. If there wasn't some type of system to it, it would spiral out of control and nothing would ever get done.

That first day left me full of questions. I returned a few days later, again helping out on the ground and getting in a minute here and there to pick Tracy's brain. After lunch, as I was moving horses around and helping saddle up, Tracy approached me with a saddled horse that had two eyes unlike any I'd ever seen on a horse.

"This is Frank—Frank Sinatra. Old Blue Eyes," he said, and handed me the reins as if I were supposed to hop up for a ride. I studied Tracy's face to see if he was serious; he knew what a complete novice I was—I'd made it very clear that you could count the number of times I'd cantered on one hand.

"My daughter [five-year-old Emma Rae] rides this horse," he answered to my expression.

"The last time I heard that, I got in *real* trouble," I said, remembering the gravel pile summitting experience at the farm where Sokeri came from.

Tracy chuckled, but didn't hang out to chat. He just handed me the reins and went back to business in the barn. I looked at Frank. The horse seemed fine with this situation. My desire to ride and try my luck in the saddle outweighed my concern for making a complete idiot of myself in front of people who surely would notice, so forward I went.

I knew from my natural horsemanship training that a little groundwork is always a good thing before mounting. I took the left rein and began to bend Frank's head towards me to get lateral flexion—of course I didn't have the chance to go through my normal twenty-minute routine, but I figured at least a little pressure-and-release activity couldn't hurt. Frank seemed confused for just a second, then turned his head slightly. As I asked for him to come further with the flexion he stepped towards me in the front. He had no idea what I was asking. So, I figured I'd not confuse him and just hop into the saddle the way these folks did, breaking one of those cardinal NH rules.

Frank stood fine as I mounted (which every horse had for each rider all morning long). I sat a minute getting settled, then lightly picked up the split reins in one hand and with the tiniest movement of them towards my belly Old Blue Eyes softly and immediately backed. Then I steered toward the open round-pen gate. It was my first neck-reining experience, and it was like driving a horse with a joystick. Frank moved his front end around, straightened up, and then walked easily over and through the gate. I'd never ridden such a light and finished horse. Literally, I needed only to think what I wanted to do next, and Frank was there for me. We walked, moved the front end around, stopped, backed, and walked again. "It's like power steering!" Tracy called over to me, appearing suddenly from behind the web of bridles by the gate and breaking the spell I was in. He wasn't kidding.

The front quarters moved much like those of my horses, with cues from the reins and legs. Reverse was there. Frank, however, did not bend his head laterally more than a couple of inches before engaging the front and stepping. After further exploration of the various cues I'd learned with horses, I discovered he knew nothing of disengaging the hindquarters. I found a diplomatic way of asking Tracy about this without giving away my "horse hugger" background. "I noticed Frank doesn't move his hindquarters the way my mare does."

"I don't want the horse's hind to move!" he exclaimed. "The front is a turning mechanism; the rear is a propulsion and stopping mechanism. Do this: go ahead and back him holding the reins in your left hand."

We started backwards.

"Now reach down with your right hand, take the rein, and steer to the right."

I barely moved the right rein. I was completely unprepared for the g forces. Frank pivoted on his hind end and sprang forward in the new direction so quickly I almost ended up in the sand. It was unbelievable! "Wow!" I shouted as a reflex, my heart pounding. When I had gathered myself, I looked over to see Tracy laughing. I just grinned from ear to ear and did it again—prepared this time—then again to the left.

It was then it occurred to me that horses with a particular job can have specific training, yet still be soft throughout, and wickedly responsive. A part of me still believes that thorough NH training, which allows all possible ranges of motion, might present more overall options and therefore be best for horse and rider. But that could just be arrogance, and there is a good argument that a horse with a specific task like cutting may need only some ranges of this motion. It's just a different way of thinking. And Frank was one fine horse!

At this point I was the only rider in the round pen, but along the fence that made up the perimeter, two huge old cows lay in the deep masonry-sand footing chewing their cud. These are the "babysitters" that help keep the younger cattle calm while they are in the pen for cutting practice. A Paint and an Appaloosa were tied about thirty feet apart at the far side of the pen. Tracy explained that they represented the "hold-back" riders who are present during competition to keep the herd at bay while the cutter cuts one out and shows the finesse of horse and rider at keeping it from re-turning to that herd. Two other mounted riders, making a total of five people at work during a cutting competition, work opposite the cutter to keep the singled-out cow pressed towards him. With the whole pen to myself except for the two tied, sleepy-eyed horses and two fat bovines, I worked on loping a little. I tried to get into the rhythm of Frank's movements. I was semi-successful.

Adam, one of Tracy's employees, entered on a stallion to lope. They circled me a few times cantering. Then he said to me, "Go up and bring out six or seven."

Gulp. Had I heard him right? Go into the holding pens and bring out fresh cattle? I looked at him as he cantered by again. He seemed serious. My total riding time on a horse couldn't have been more than twenty hours at that time, but I was having a re-ally good time and figured what the heck! Besides, I figured Frank had to know what he was doing.

We went to the gate, I leaned over and opened it, and Frank and I entered a chute with several gates leading to holding pens with young cattle. I chose the gate that looked like it held the eas-iest, best behaved cows, leaned over from the saddle, and opened it. I asked Frank to enter and he calmly stepped inside and worked easily around the cows we needed, then pushed them qui-etly through the gate into the chute. I closed the gate from the saddle and then moved the cows the rest of the way into the round pen. It was the most fun I had had since shooting out a candle flame in the dark with a rifle at two hundred yards!

Tracy, for all his rapid-fire, seemingly chaotic activity, never missed a thing around that place. "Push them over between those horses," he shouted from somewhere unseen. So Frank and I did. "Make those old cows get up and get over there too," he added, now visible over by a tack rack with the cell phone to his ear. Frank followed my lead right on over and then seemed to have a bit of fun pushing in close at the babysitters' space to get them onto their feet. Then the pros started entering the round pen and I had to give up my triumphant moment and my mount.

Tracy has generously shared much information and time with me. In the big picture of my natural horsemanship progress as a beginner, he deserves a chapter if for no other reason than one big lesson: natural horse folk don't corner the market on good horsemanship. But there are a number of points I have to make on that statement which will no doubt ruffle a few feathers.

First, many great horse folk over the years have come to an understanding of gentle ways of working with horses without giving their methods any particular name; it's just how they have done it. These days you can follow Parelli, Lyons, Brannaman, Neubert, Campbell, or whoever . . . all of whom generally get placed under the umbrella of "natural horsemanship," and still you will come out with that many different approaches to working with horses—some even opposing one another. Why should it be so surprising that perhaps other folks who haven't been categorized at all wouldn't have good approaches as well?

It is unquestionably Tom Dorrance and his amazing work with many good hands, particularly Ray Hunt, that have provided the nucleus for what Dr. Miller and Rick Lamb call *The Revolution in Horsemanship* (they feel so strongly about it being an actual revolution that it is the title of their recent book). But Dorrance isn't the only starting point for every good horseman, although it's likely every good horseman respects his achievements and way with horses.

Considering the Horse, a book by popular clinician Mark Rashid, provides a great example of what I mean. In this book Rashid tells the story of how he came to learn what he has developed into a brilliant understanding of working gently with horses. The lessons for him began with a teacher whom he refers to as "the old man," a fellow by the name of Walter Pruitt. This patient, chain-smoking mentor guided Rashid as a young boy to work with horses by seeing things from the horse's perspective. Rashid confirmed for me that the old man lived in Wisconsin and never had any dealings with Tom Dorrance, so Rashid's entry into the movement is from a source altogether different from many clinicians and trainers. After a good leg-up from his mentor, Rashid learned a tremendous amount from horses themselves, just working through situation after situation, which required a certain amount of open-mindedness and willingness to see things from the horse's perspective. It may be that all great horse folk get a start somehow, probably with a human somewhere along the way, but then become great by understanding the lessons horses give them directly.

Another example is Harry Whitney. He is considered part of the natural horsemanship movement, yet his renowned ability to "see things from the horse's point of view" came from direct experience. Whitney came out of the rodeo life, where he spent years performing tricks with a variety of animals, including horses, and developed his own style of horsemanship. His means and words may differ from others, and he never studied under anyone, and yet his work overlaps and has common ground with the horsemen who derive from Dorrance.

Horse folk firmly seated in the natural horsemanship movement don't have a complete monopoly on working well with horses, and there are even greatly varying approaches within the movement itself. Many of these folks would tell you that themselves. Actually, my experience with a number of fine clinicians is that they don't care for the categorization. The term "natural horsemanship" itself bothers a great many of them, and many don't personally use it to describe what they do. This lumping together and allotting of titles may be more for mass convenience than truly revealing of just what approach to training is going on. In reality, lumping together certain horse folk under the heading "natural horsemanship" may be helpful towards understanding what's going on when we look at the big horse picture, but what it actually *means* is a real question open to quite a bit of interpretation.

So I present as evidence to the argument several quotes from my friend and brilliant mainstream trainer Tracy Barton:

"I've got to let the horses want *to do it."*

"Cutting is a mental game even more than a physical game."

"Time off for the horses to 'recharge the batteries' is critical."

"Man-made problems in horses stem from having too much pressure put on them mentally."

"A lot of trainers make the horse fit them; I believe it's my job to fit the horse."

"I don't believe in using mechanical devices. You want a true cow horse. A horse that is going to cut no matter who rides him.

The difference between a cow horse and a show horse is that a show horse must be ridden a certain way—the trainer can take that horse out and win, but a less experienced rider can't. With a true cow horse, anyone can get on and when you drop your hand, it cuts."

Now Tracy, either by his own definition or anyone else's, does not fall into the category of natural horsemanship—he's clearly a mainstream trainer. But his way with horses is not altogether different, call it what you will. I might just call it "good horsemanship," or I might steal Mark Rashid's title and say that trainer *considers the horse*. He cares deeply for the horses in his barn, and horses in general, and it shows in his training.

Part of what the natural horsemanship movement has done is create a *language* specific to itself. Words like "disengage," "pressure and release," and "groundwork" won't be heard at the TTB, but I believe Tracy operates within the same realm of horse understanding as all great horse folk. People that develop a deep understanding of horses, regardless of category and background, understand and use similar ways of communication with them even if specialized for a specific usage—in this situation, cutting.

The last time I went down to the TTB, I had a conversation with a client of Tracy's that sums it up for me. She described how she came to find Tracy as a trainer. She had her horse with another trainer, and at every competition she attended, she kept seeing certain horses that just had something extra. This one group of people kept winning. Exploring the reason, she discovered they were all horses and riders under Tracy's tutelage. "I wanted to be in that group!" she said. She had actually moved to Virginia to be close to the TTB.

"Tracy has something different," this mainstream horse-woman said and paused, thinking hard to try and come up with a way to express it. "He . . . well, it's like . . . hmm . . . it's like he can *feel* the horse."

CHAPTER FOURTEEN

SOKERI STANDS STILL

THE CHALLENGE OF GETTING SOKERI TO STAND while I mounted took quite awhile for me to figure out. As mentioned before, I worked through it by consistently and repeatedly going through the same steps to get up into the saddle, and then stepping down and backing her a few steps from the ground each time she moved off. Even though it took a long time to establish with her, it was nothing compared to getting that horse to stand still once I was on her.

It amazed me that I finally was able to communicate that she needed to stand still for the mounting part of this process, but that I couldn't get it through for her to stand from about thirty seconds after mounting to the end of a ride. Since a lot of praising for the right thing and stepping down and backing up for the wrong thing had worked for the mounting problem, I logically tried putting her in reverse to remedy the stepping-off problem. It didn't work.

Taking her own notion to go whenever she felt the urge was so persistent that I began just by default to immediately connect with the reins and go back a few steps, once I was situated in the saddle after stepping up or mounting from the fence. She always backed easily and with a light touch. Then she'd stand a second and walk off anyway. So I'd stop and then back her. She'd stand a couple of seconds and then walk off. And so on and so forth . . . which brings me to an interesting crossroads in my understanding of horses.

Sometimes problems like this one are just a matter of communication. Simply getting better at communicating with the horse is all that is needed. If I pay closer attention to how I'm asking the horse to move, I may discover an inconsistency in my application of pressure and release. Anytime release comes at the wrong moment, it will cause confusion, and being late or early with the release is easy to do at first. Sometimes I'm guilty of starting with pressure that is too firm. Sokeri is a sensitive horse, and it doesn't usually require much to get her to understand a request. She can become a bit offended if I start with what to her is a startling amount of pressure. I must remember to do just as much as it takes, and that means a lot of concentration on my part to start with a much softer request than what comes naturally to me. In fact, remembering to start with *feel* before going to a physical pressure is really important, and I'm certainly guilty of overlooking that step and going right to mechanical cues. Starting with and maintaining the awareness of feel, though, is essential to getting better with horses.

If the horse is willing and paying attention but you can't get the horse to do what you ask, then a communication problem is likely the issue. With Sokeri, I worked hard for several months to get across to her to stand still while I'm in the saddle. Whenever she took the notion, which was frequently, off we went. I found myself even trying to guess when she was going to make a move and ask for her to go first, even if I hadn't been planning on it—a kind of preemptive strike, and not much of a real fix, I know. A horse that is in tune with the rider, where both parties are on the same page and willingly working together where the rider gets to decide when and which direction to go, is what I wanted with my horse.

Another consideration (although I know of some specific instances where this is used as a bogus excuse not to work with a horse, which I strongly disagree with) is physical problems. While not terribly common it seems, sometimes a horse not responding to your request could be due to physical discomfort. If you know your horse, you should pick up on an unusual resistance to a request as an abnormal situation and figure out what is up. If you are breaking new ground on a horse you don't know and have problems, you just have to check out areas that might be causing him pain. It is a good thing to keep in mind because, just like it would be with you, if some physical problem exists, forcing the horse into a painful position will have negative results.

I rode a buckskin Quarter Horse used as a turn-back horse during some cutting training recently. The horse was experienced, neck-reined like a dream, responded to the slightest cue, and loved his cow work. I noticed, however, that he got a little agitated when I'd try to bend him to the left. As supple as this horse was in the other direction, it seemed really odd, especially when he went so far as to throw his head around when I'd try to move his front quarters to the left. I figured, as is often the case when I ride cutting horses, that it was just the difference between mainstream broke horses and the alternatively trained horses I work with most of the time. The imbalance from one side to the other, however, was so odd that I asked one of the regular hands there about it. He explained the horse had broken two vertebrae in his neck when he was younger, so he was retired from cutting to turning back. That explained a lot, and I was able to allow for that physical limitation when riding and get on with business in fine style from that point on.

Then there is the braced horse. This gets into some pretty difficult territory for me and inexperienced horse folk at large. The brace can be a physical manifestation of a mental problem. Horses can remember traumatic experiences, and these may create stress, which comes out as a rigidness somewhere in the horse's body, like a stiff leg, for instance. I've watched Bill Scott work with a horse at a clinic to check out whether its bracing problem was mental or actually a physical difficulty (it can be really hard to figure out; in that case he went through numerous groundwork exercises and determined the horse was mentally braced, but that was guru level stuff and I couldn't tell exactly what he saw). Generally speaking, working through the mental brace requires supporting the horse emotionally while pushing him beyond the hang-up. The horse is convinced it can't do what you are asking of him. Once you prove to him that he can, often the brace simply dissolves and you achieve a great breakthrough.

None of this, however, was the case with Sokeri. It became more obvious to me as I worked with Niji that her not standing still issue was one that fell into the respect category.

The lesson I got from Terrie more than a year earlier about firming up with Sokeri on the lead rope during groundwork went through my mind as I considered her wandering off. She would never do this to me on the ground; she stayed planted until I asked her to move in that scenario. By this point in our relationship, even in an open pasture, if I approached, she'd stop whatever she was doing, turn to face me, and stay put until I walked away. Once I was on her back, however, the respect was getting lost. This is, of course, unacceptable in general and potentially dangerous. Some clinicians say their relationship with the horse is 49 percent the horse and 51 percent them as the rider. That seems like an okay policy as long as that 49 percent doesn't include deciding when we're going to move and where—it's not an open invitation to just do whatever nearly half the time. It should be reserved for *Watch out for that rattlesnake*, or, *This gravel is killing my feet, may we please walk on the grassy edge of the road?*

One of the more frustrating truths about getting better with horses relates to something I was told by several people early on: "Some things you hear or read from the great horsemen you won't understand until the time is right; then they will click into place." This can be days, weeks, months, or even years later. *What kind of bull is that?* was my thinking when I'd hear it, but it has been proven to me several times now. This was just such an instance.

The Bill Scott clinic (yes, the one featuring the now-famous Tom-goes-through-the-fence wreck) planted a very important seed in my head that would later germinate and grow into a really important understanding. As I closely watched Bill interacting with Niji in the round pen, a new awareness struck me. Bill asked

Niji to pay attention to him, to turn and face him and keep both eyes on him. Niji would at first, but then digressed and turned his attention elsewhere. Bill gave him an opportunity to come back with both eyes, and when the gelding ignored the good deal, Bill sent him around the round pen. It became the horse's choice. How badly does the horse want to be still? It seems so simple, but this was a lightning bolt striking me right in the brain, and in that round pen setting I truly grasped the significance of it. What I didn't know was that it would be the basis for so many more really important breakthroughs for me with my horses in the future.

I was home and worked daily with Sokeri for over a month after that clinic. She walked off with me on her back whenever she felt like it, all the while I backed her, saying "Whoa," having serious one-on-one discussions in plain English, and whatever else I could come up with. One day that seed of Bill's teaching

Sokeri and I go for a trail ride, and Whipper Snapper decides to tag along.

took root in my consciousness and sprouted into something new. The reason it finally occurred to me is still a mystery, but one day as I was preparing to ride Sokeri in a large pasture where Niji and Whipper Snapper also were, it just became clear: I didn't have Sokeri's respect when in the saddle in the same way Bill didn't have Niji's respect at first in the round pen. Then, shouldn't the answer to the problem be the same?

So often the solutions to problems with horses are not complex. It seems there really isn't some enigmatic secret to overcoming difficulties with our equine partners. Most often the fix is just applying a fundamental of good horsemanship in the right way. And notice here, that by definition, this means that the *human* just hadn't put it together. Really, even with only a few years of experience with horses, it is clear to me that horses react consistently. They don't mislead others. They don't lie. They are incapable of deception—it isn't part of their makeup. It seems they even experience relief when a person finally gets it right and the horse/human relationship improves. After all, their lives also get easier when the feel begins to flow.

The round pen answer to Niji's respect issue was to "make the right thing easy," a concept I had heard over and over since probably the second day of discovering the Better Way with horses. Making the right thing easy for Niji in the round corral meant that when his attention was on Bill, he had release from any pressure; the gelding could just stand easy. But, if his attention wandered, Bill gave him ample opportunity with soft requests to tune back in, and if Niji didn't, Bill applied pressure to move the horse's feet. After sending him around, he would release that pressure and get Niji to stop, turn, and give his undivided attention. As long as Niji stayed focused on Bill, he had it easy. Every time his attention wandered off, he consistently received Bill's pressure to move his feet and head out around the corral. It only took a couple of times for that bright horse to get it figured out, and he chose to stand and look at that cowboy in his big straw hat and chaps rather than trot around in the heat for the opportunity to gaze over the fence at some mare grazing nearby. If this method worked so well with Niji in that circumstance, couldn't I *make Sokeri move her feet more than she intended to whenever she went to move them on her own*?

Counterintuitive? You betcha. Here I was trying to get her to stand still, but instead of trying to get her to stand still when she moved on her own, I'm going to make her move more energetically than she intended whenever she decides to move without being asked. It seemed crazy and yet made sense to me when put in the round corral context.

Trying the theory was easy, I just mounted her and counted to seven. She stepped off, and I was ready. Instead of stopping and backing like the other fifteen thousand times she'd done this, I immediately popped her up to a trot. Then we cantered. Then we zigzagged at high speeds. Then we transitioned down to a walk and stopped.

She stood there for a moment, nostrils flaring. I rose and fell with her deep breaths. She must have wondered where the heck that unusual burst of craziness came from. Then, instead of just standing still and relaxing, which would have been fine with me, she chose to take a step, and BOOM! I upped the energy from the saddle and off we went to the races again. Riding like the wind was a great time for me, but she was having to work hard.

I'm here to tell you that her stepping off problem was completely cured in fifteen minutes of this. She clearly understood in no uncertain terms that if she chose to be still, she avoided me going into Mario Andretti mode. Soke quickly learned to make the easy choice. To this day, some six months hence, she stands contentedly when I'm aboard and has not moved off once until I ask since then. That's a pretty amazing result. A few days later, before I knew for sure it had stuck, I had the opportunity to ask Ray Hunt about the validity of my experiment when I met him at a clinic in Virginia.

The best lesson from working through this problem with Sokeri hasn't been learning a great trick to get a horse to stand still, though. Rather, it is a new way of thinking that has myriad applications with horses and in other parts of life. Often, we have all the tools we need to solve a problem—we just need to regroup and see things in a new light or arrange the pieces that are in front of us together in a new way. With horses, when I get stuck now (which is constantly, because I'm always trying to get better with them and do new things), I go back through what I've learned and ask basic questions to seek answers. If I can't communicate something, I always look at how I'm asking first. Am I starting with a soft enough feel? Am I consistently upping the pressure in the same way each time? Am I willing to follow through on the request? Does my action actually communicate what I seek? Does the horse give me his attention? Do I need to go back through some really basic groundwork and pay close attention to see if there's a sticking point somewhere I missed? And, of course, am I making the right thing easy?

These questions have become the very basis of my daily life with horses. The value of new applications of basic techniques, like those Bill Scott took time out of his day to share with me and Niji in that round pen, is still unfolding.

CHAPTER FIFTEEN

THE END OF THE BEGINNING

IT'S NEARLY IMPOSSIBLE TO LEARN much about the Better Way with horses without hearing the name Ray Hunt. If you polled the best horse folk in the country as to who is the greatest living horseman, Ray Hunt would likely be a unanimous winner. Actually, in 2005, when *Western Horseman* magazine produced a Horseman of the Year issue, Hunt was the first to receive the accolade, proving this very point and landing a close-up of his face on the cover.

Hunt learned directly from Tom Dorrance and is largely responsible through his clinics for getting Dorrance's methods out on the road and into the consciousness of the broader horse world. In a large way, the natural horsemanship movement has Hunt to thank for being a movement at all, rather than a few folks out west just sharing a really great way of dealing with horses among themselves.

Even with time ticking on and a health issue or two in the past few years, Hunt keeps up his clinic schedule. On the second and third of April 2005, there was a big gathering in Fort Worth, Texas, to honor the great horseman. The guest list may have made it the single greatest gathering of capable horse folk ever assembled in one place in the history of the world. I thought it indicated that Hunt might be winding down from the rigors of the road and performing clinics. It never occurred to me that I might have an opportunity to meet and learn from him directly. But, as this new direction in my life with horses opened up, suddenly and unexpectedly it led straight to Ray Hunt—who, by the way, apparently isn't about to quit his job.

A few months after the Bill Scott clinic, some of the local natural horse enthusiasts got together for a semi-regular video night. I'd wanted to go in the past, but something always came up to prevent it. I was able to make this one. The video was of Buck Brannaman doing some groundwork. Amazingly, it was one I hadn't seen before. Afterwards, conversation started up, and I nearly dropped my cheese cracker when one of the women mentioned she was going to northern Virginia in a couple of weeks to see a Ray Hunt clinic.

"WHAT?" was my reaction. I interrupted her conversation right then to see if I'd heard right. I had. I couldn't believe it! Ray Hunt in Virginia. I was determined right then to grab this opportunity to see the legendary horseman in action. For the horse enthusiast of the Better Way, the chance to see Ray Hunt is like a stand-up comedian getting to attend a comedy workshop hosted by Bob Hope. I immediately went home and told Carol, but she had to be in Richmond at that time and wouldn't be able to go with me. I contacted the host for the event and learned that the farm where it would be held was only an hour and a half from where Ken and Melissa lived in Maryland. It was a five-hour drive for me, but I called Ken and we chiseled in stone our plans to meet there.

It was a Saturday, and it was also Kentucky Derby day. I set the clock for 3 a.m. and was on the road by 3:30. I arrived a little ahead of the rush of attendees. The day was cool, but clear. I paid my fee and walked around checking out several of the horses coming off trailers to participate in the clinic. Ken and Melissa got there not long after I did, as did three women from the video night. We all set up folding chairs right next to the round pen and waited to see the colt starting action.

"I'm here for the horse," Hunt made clear when he entered the round pen first thing that morning. It's a disclaimer you'd better pay attention to. He's not kidding.

Hunt is much less concerned about hurting someone's feelings than improving situations for horses. If a horse is having trouble, it's a human-made problem as far as he's concerned. Sure, he can fix it by working with the horse, but then that horse has to leave and return home to the same person it has been with all along. Long-term benefit to the horse only comes through real change in the person who works with the horse. So Hunt says exactly what he thinks about the problem's origins and just what the human has done to create it in the hope of getting to the root of it—even if the person is standing right there in front of a hundred spectators. A person able to accept and learn from this sometimes harsh reality check can improve dramatically from such a teacher. One more thin-skinned might be quite offended. If someone shuts down or stomps off, he probably wouldn't be a likely candidate to take an improved horse home and support the positive changes anyway—so Hunt gives it to you straight, right from his first sentence of the clinic.

Hunt is also a man of few words, it seemed to me. Much of that morning, he worked with colts in the round pen, most saddled only a time or two before the experience. Typically, two would be saddled and put into the round pen, with him in the center. Hunt would connect with these youngsters by a look or gesture or invisible telepathy. Every so often, he might pick up the flag and shake it just a bit to get a change in the colts. For many that morning, he moved them around a time or two and then said, "All right, these are good, bring me in a couple more." I watched so intently to see just what the master did in that round pen that my brain just plain hurt after awhile. I wanted to catch exactly what he saw in each colt, and then just exactly what he did when he saw whatever he saw. One of the lessons of that day I was already figuring out on my path to the horse—that you often can't *see* what it is that makes a person a good hand with horses; therefore it can't be mimicked from just watching. It's that elusive *feel* showing up again. That is one thing that really puts video at a disadvantage as a teaching tool with horses.

Hunt always answered questions when asked. It seems, if knowing something is important enough to you to ask, he's more than happy to meet you halfway and try his best to answer. If, on the other hand, you can't bring yourself to ask a question, he's not particularly inclined to go out of his way to stop you and tell you what you need to do to improve. He's not the type to just go on endlessly talking about what he's doing while he works with a horse or go looking for problems all around the arena to fix for examples. Sometimes he puts his two cents in while working with a horse, but just as often it seems he quietly works through something in his own silent way.

I'm guessing from my experience that day that Hunt is more apt to let people discover things on their own, as lessons born of firsthand experience are more likely to stick. While he was work-ing the colts that morning, I had a thousand questions. The dif-ficulty was asking only the most important ones and not hogging the session. In particular, I asked him about what indications he saw in the colts he was working that let him know they were ready to move on to the next stage and leave the round pen. "Sometimes," I carefully formed my question, hoping not to sound like an idiot, "I can see the obvious signs in these colts that I would expect, like turning an ear towards you, or stopping to face you relaxed. But other times, and I've been watching real closely, I see no difference or change whatsoever. But you see that they're ready to go on. How do you know?"

His smile, at once showing amusement and understanding, said it all—and the answer he gave amounted to "I just know." Sometimes a colt reveals his inner state in an outward way that can be interpreted and discussed among onlookers. Sometimes not. Hunt knows either way. And he doesn't have to force the colt to show certain outward postures if the inner workings are al-ready good. For him, it goes back to being there for the colt first, not necessarily about trying to see if he can get everyone to understand what he's doing or what he observes with each one in that round corral. But, since I asked, he did give some insight and explained that he was interacting with the colts and looking for issues people have built into these young horses, even at an early stage. The dozen he saw that morning, ranging from Quarters to Belgians and even a couple of mules, he admitted, all looked real good and had no big problems that needed sorting out.

Once I heard someone make a statement about Ray Hunt that, when I repeat it, always gets a laugh from those who have firsthand knowledge of him. "It's a good thing Ray Hunt isn't a swimming instructor," it goes, "because if he was, half his students would drown!"

It's funny, but mostly because it's true. And, I'd have to add, it's true because some students don't make the effort to swim, which is hardly Hunt's fault. If you come to a clinic to learn to swim, jump in the water, and let yourself sink to the bottom and just stay there—well, OK, there you have it: lungs full of water. I think when you get right down to it, a lot of humans want to have things done for them. They expect magically to reap some benefit without putting in the work it takes to get it done. I think that's why advertisements for exercise machines are rivaled in number only by exercise machines seen in yard sales and dumps.

I'm dead sure some folks want their horse to improve, hear a good clinician is coming to town, pay the money, take the horse and think, *Well, five hundred bucks with a great trainer ought to get this horse over these bad habits.* The thing is, the horse is reflecting just what the human has done with it. I'd bet Hunt knows he could fix any problem in any horse at any of his clinics, but that there's no good in doing that unless the person that works with that horse also improves. He could have improved every horse in that clinic that day, sent them home, and a day later it would all be undone if the people didn't improve what *they* were capable of doing with those horses.

Towards the end of the colt starting part of the clinic, I heard Hunt say, "You have to give something you never gave to get something you never had." I even stopped what I was doing and wrote it down so I wouldn't forget it. If that requires a nonswimmer to choke on some water to figure out he's got to start moving his arms to swim, well, so be it—he won't likely forget that lesson, and he'll always be the better for it. If he just drowns, well, maybe he just wasn't cut out to be a swimmer. It's tough love for humans and total love for horses with Ray Hunt.

The afternoon switched to a riding session in a large outdoor arena. Hunt had the group start with a simple task—riding in a single-file oval around the edge of the arena, with equal spacing between horses. This instantly brought problems to the surface. Really, to be honest, after about thirty seconds it looked like a chaotic mess that sort of moved counterclockwise. I could tell

Ray Hunt—the man who's here for the horse.

three of the twenty riders could have done it easily, another couple could have managed with considerable effort if they were alone in there with those first capable three. The rest were all over the place. While it would have been easy to sit on the sidelines, point a finger, and think, *Gosh, these people can't even do that?* with a smirk, I didn't delude myself. I knew from firsthand experience it can take two clinic days even to get on a horse, let alone *ride* one without having a wreck in the arena.

As far as maneuvers go, the afternoon hours never showed progress much beyond horses moving in ovals at a walk or trot. Hunt began to work in some advice here and there to shape up different riders with varying degrees of success. Ken and I sat in our folding chairs watching, talking about what we saw, and having a great time. He got up once to shoot some pictures of the clinic from different angles.

After the clinic ended, it cleared out amazingly fast. I figured this was likely due to people wanting to catch the Derby. Hunt went over to the round pen, where he watched a woman ride and gave her some advice. Then I was able to have a few minutes to speak with him.

At this point with Sokeri, I had just gotten her to begin standing still when I was in the saddle by making her move out fast when she stepped off without being asked. That tactic had occurred to me and had not been suggested, so I'd had no professional feedback about it. This was the first opportunity I'd had to bounce it off a knowledgeable clinician of the Better Way to see if it was the right thing to do. It just happened to be Ray Hunt.

I explained my problem with Sokeri walking off all the time, then my thought process behind my solution, and then the fact that the result was positive and really fast coming. "So . . . " I finished my explanation, "what about that approach?"

"You did exactly right," he replied.

Now to some, this statement might not seem like much. Many would see this as simply the answer to a question. To me, however, having Ray Hunt acknowledge that I had worked for over a month on a problem with my horse, finally applied the basic principles of natural horsemanship in a unique way, figuring it out all on my own, gotten results, and done "exactly right" was the end of the beginning. My odyssey as a beginner in the world of natural horsemanship clearly began with Niji; likewise in my mind, it clearly ended with Ray Hunt's words that day.

I still can't profess to be much more than a beginner, but from that moment on, it occurred to me that I was getting somewhere . . . where exactly, I wasn't sure, but if Ray Hunt said, "You did exactly right," regarding that matter with Sokeri, I *was* getting better with horses. And, it was somewhere beyond being a total novice.

AFTERWORD

I SMILED FOR A WEEK, or maybe a month. Then, after months more—long after I was confident I had solved the stepping off problem—Sokeri started stepping off again for no apparent reason. As much as I'd like to not admit this fact and leave things wrapped up in a nice tidy way, it is the truth.

And that's how it really goes with horses, even with the Better Way. Just when you think you've got it together with a horse, the horse is ready to challenge you again. They are great at it, and now I'm certain it is always that way with horses. It is, at the very least, the truth about how things go with horses and me. Perhaps the greatest lesson horses can teach us is that life is a process. It is a never-ending search to improve. In the quest to get better with horses, no matter how capable we become, they will forever present new challenges for us to work through.

This time, my brilliant fix that worked before didn't work. Why? I wish I knew. So, what did I do? At this point, I'm still working on it. Good thing I'm not a beginner anymore. So, I wonder, what would Ray Hunt do about this?

ABOUT THE AUTHOR

TOM MOATES IS A PROFESSIONAL WRITER driving most of the people in his life nuts as he obsessively tries to get better with horses. For a decade Moates was a leading writer in the country on the subjects of homesteading and renewable energy when he was suddenly and hopelessly smitten with horses. His life and writing both took sharp turns, as chronicled in this book, and now he is a major figure in equine magazine writing. He is a contributing writer at *Equus* and writes regularly for *Eclectic Horseman* and *Western Horseman*. His work also appears in many other national and regional horse magazines including *The American Quarter Horse Journal* and *Natural Horse*. Moates lives in southwest Virginia on a solar-powered farm with his wife, Carol, along with three horses and a mule. Visit him on the Web at www.TomMoates.com.

PHOTO CREDITS